John Dewey's Democracy and Education in an Era of Globalization

2016 marked the hundred-year anniversary of John Dewey's seminal work *Democracy and Education*. This centennial presented philosophers and educators with an opportunity to reexamine and evaluate its impact on various aspects of education in democratic societies. This volume brings together some of the leading scholars on John Dewey and education from around the world in order to reflect on the legacy of *Democracy and Education*, and, more generally, to consider the influence of Dewey's ideas on education in the twenty-first century. *John Dewey's Democracy and Education in an Era of Globalization* is unique in that it explores some important tensions and relationships among Dewey's ideas on democracy, education, and human flourishing in an era of globalization. The contributors make sense of how Dewey would have interpreted and responded to the phenomenon of globalization.

This book was originally published as a special issue of *Educational Philosophy and Theory*.

Mordechai Gordon is a Professor of Education in the School of Education at Quinnipiac University, USA. His areas of specialization are the philosophy of education, democratic education and humor. He is the author of six books and numerous articles in scholarly journals such as *Educational Theory*, *Journal of Teacher Education*, *Oxford Review of Education* and *Journal of Aesthetic Education*.

Andrea R. English is Chancellor's Fellow in Philosophy of Education at the Moray House School of Education, University of Edinburgh, UK, and Senior Fellow of the Higher Education Academy. She is author of *Discontinuity in Learning: Dewey, Herbart, and Education as Transformation* (2013), co-editor of *John Dewey's Democracy and Education: A Centennial Handbook* (2017), and her research on teaching and learning has been published in a range of international journals and edited volumes.

Educational Philosophy and Theory
Series Editor: Peter Roberts, University of Canterbury, New Zealand

This series is devoted to cutting-edge scholarship in educational philosophy and theory. Each book in the series focuses on a key theme or thinker and includes essays from a range of contributors. To be published in the series, a book will normally have first appeared as a special issue of *Educational Philosophy and Theory*, one of the premier philosophy of education journals in the world. This provides an assurance for readers of the quality of the work and enhances the visibility of the book in the international philosophy of education community. Books in this series combine creativity with rigour and insight. The series is intended to demonstrate the value of diverse theoretical perspectives in educational discourse, and contributors are invited to draw on literature, art and film as well as traditional philosophical sources in their work. Questions of educational policy and practice will also be addressed. The books published in this series will provide key reference points for subsequent theoretical work by other scholars, and will play a significant role in advancing philosophy of education as a field of study.

Titles in the series include:

Philosophy and Pedagogy of Early Childhood
Edited by Sandy Farquhar and E. Jayne White

The Dilemma of Western Philosophy
Edited by Michael A. Peters and Carl Mika

Educational Philosophy and New French Thought
Edited by David R. Cole and Joff P.N. Bradley

Activating Aesthetics
Edited by Elizabeth M. Grierson

Levinas and the Philosophy of Education
Edited by Guoping Zhao

The Confucian Concept of Learning
Revisited for East Asian Humanistic Pedagogies
Edited by Duck-Joo Kwak, Morimichi Kato and Ruyu Hung

A Kaleidoscopic View of Chinese Philosophy of Education
Edited by Ruyu Hung

John Dewey's Democracy and Education in an Era of Globalization
Edited by Mordechai Gordon and Andrea R. English

John Dewey's Democracy and Education in an Era of Globalization

Edited by
**Mordechai Gordon and
Andrea R. English**

LONDON AND NEW YORK

First published 2018
by Routledge
2 Park Square, Milton Park, Abingdon, Oxon, OX14 4RN, UK

and by Routledge
711 Third Avenue, New York, NY 10017, USA

Routledge is an imprint of the Taylor & Francis Group, an informa business

© 2018 Philosophy of Education Society of Australasia

All rights reserved. No part of this book may be reprinted or reproduced or utilised in any form or by any electronic, mechanical, or other means, now known or hereafter invented, including photocopying and recording, or in any information storage or retrieval system, without permission in writing from the publishers.

Trademark notice: Product or corporate names may be trademarks or registered trademarks, and are used only for identification and explanation without intent to infringe.

British Library Cataloguing in Publication Data
A catalogue record for this book is available from the British Library

ISBN13: 978-0-8153-6250-0

Typeset in Plantin
by RefineCatch Limited, Bungay, Suffolk

Publisher's Note
The publisher accepts responsibility for any inconsistencies that may have arisen during the conversion of this book from journal articles to book chapters, namely the possible inclusion of journal terminology.

Disclaimer
Every effort has been made to contact copyright holders for their permission to reprint material in this book. The publishers would be grateful to hear from any copyright holder who is not here acknowledged and will undertake to rectify any errors or omissions in future editions of this book.

Contents

Citation Information ix
Notes on Contributors xi

Introduction: John Dewey's *Democracy and Education* in an Era of Globalization 1
Mordechai Gordon and Andrea R. English

1. Globalization, Democracy, and Social Movements: The educational potential of activism 5
Kathy Hytten

2. Complexity and Reductionism in Educational Philosophy—John Dewey's Critical Approach in 'Democracy and Education' Reconsidered 21
Kersten Reich, Jim Garrison and Stefan Neubert

3. Not 'democratic education' but 'democracy and education': Reconsidering Dewey's oft misunderstood introduction to the philosophy of education 37
John Quay

4. Thinking my way back to you: John Dewey on the communication and formation of concepts 53
Megan J. Laverty

5. John Dewey and the Role of the Teacher in a Globalized World: Imagination, empathy, and 'third voice' 70
Andrea R. English

6. American philosophy and its Eastern strains: Crisis, resilience, and self-transcendence 89
Naoko Saito

7. Why Should Scholars Keep Coming Back to John Dewey? 101
Mordechai Gordon

Index 117

Citation Information

The chapters in this book were originally published in *Educational Philosophy and Theory*, volume 48, issue 10 (September 2016). When citing this material, please use the original page numbering for each article, as follows:

Introduction
John Dewey's Democracy and Education in an Era of Globalization
Mordechai Gordon and Andrea R. English
Educational Philosophy and Theory, volume 48, issue 10 (September 2016) pp. 977–980

Chapter 1
Globalization, Democracy, and Social Movements: The educational potential of activism
Kathy Hytten
Educational Philosophy and Theory, volume 48, issue 10 (September 2016) pp. 981–996

Chapter 2
Complexity and Reductionism in Educational Philosophy — John Dewey's Critical Approach in 'Democracy and Education' Reconsidered
Kersten Reich, Jim Garrison and Stefan Neubert
Educational Philosophy and Theory, volume 48, issue 10 (September 2016) pp. 997–1012

Chapter 3
Not 'democratic education' but 'democracy and education': Reconsidering Dewey's oft misunderstood introduction to the philosophy of education
John Quay
Educational Philosophy and Theory, volume 48, issue 10 (September 2016) pp. 1013–1028

Chapter 4
Thinking my way back to you: John Dewey on the communication and formation of concepts
Megan J. Laverty
Educational Philosophy and Theory, volume 48, issue 10 (September 2016) pp. 1029–1045

CITATION INFORMATION

Chapter 5
John Dewey and the Role of the Teacher in a Globalized World: Imagination, empathy, and 'third voice'
Andrea R. English
Educational Philosophy and Theory, volume 48, issue 10 (September 2016) pp. 1046–1064

Chapter 6
American philosophy and its Eastern strains: Crisis, resilience, and self-transcendence
Naoko Saito
Educational Philosophy and Theory, volume 48, issue 10 (September 2016) pp. 1065–1076

Chapter 7
Why Should Scholars Keep Coming Back to John Dewey?
Mordechai Gordon
Educational Philosophy and Theory, volume 48, issue 10 (September 2016) pp. 1077–1091

For any permission-related enquiries please visit:
http://www.tandfonline.com/page/help/permissions

Notes on Contributors

Andrea R. English is Chancellor's Fellow in Philosophy of Education at the Moray House School of Education, University of Edinburgh, UK, and Senior Fellow of the Higher Education Academy. She is author of *Discontinuity in Learning: Dewey, Herbart, and Education as Transformation* (2013), co-editor of *John Dewey's Democracy and Education: A Centennial Handbook* (2017), and her research on teaching and learning has been published in a range of international journals and edited volumes.

Jim Garrison is Professor of Philosophy of Education at Virginia Tech University, USA. He is the author of *John Dewey's Philosophy of Education* (with Neubert and Reich, 2012), and *Living and Learning* (2014), a dialogue with Larry Hickman and Daisaku Ikeda, which initially appeared in Japanese, but has now been translated into English.

Mordechai Gordon is a Professor of Education in the School of Education at Quinnipiac University, USA. His areas of specialization are the philosophy of education, democratic education and humor. He is the author of six books and numerous articles in scholarly journals such as *Educational Theory*, *Journal of Teacher Education*, *Oxford Review of Education* and *Journal of Aesthetic Education*.

Kathy Hytten is a Professor in the Department of Educational Leadership and Cultural Foundations at the University of North Carolina at Greensboro, USA. She specializes in philosophy and sociology of education, and her research seeks to uncover systematic inequities, creating more empowering alternative educational and social practices.

Megan J. Laverty is Associate Professor of Philosophy and Education at Teachers College, Columbia University, USA. Her primary research interests are philosophy of education, moral philosophy, and pre-college philosophy. She is the editor of *Art's Teachings, Teaching's Arts: Philosophical, Critical and Educational Musings* (with Tyson E. Lewis, 2015) and *In Community of Inquiry with Ann Margaret Sharp: Philosophy, Childhood and Education* (with Maughn Gregory, 2017).

John Quay is Associate Professor in the Graduate School of Education, University of Melbourne, Australia. His research interests include philosophy of education, curriculum theory, physical education, outdoor education, and environmental education. To these interests he brings an understanding of the philosophical works of Dewey, Heidegger, and Peirce.

NOTES ON CONTRIBUTORS

Stefan Neubert is a Professor at the University of Köln, Germany, where he is the director of the Center for International Relations and co-director of the Dewey-Center. His research focuses on constructivism in education, democracy and education, Deweyan pragmatism, and intercultural education. His books include *Democracy and Education Reconsidered* (2016).

Kersten Reich is a Professor at the University of Köln, Germany, where he is director of the Dewey-Center. He is also the founder of the Interactive Constructivism, a brand of constructivism that is culturally orientated and stands in close proximity with pragmatism (especially Deweyan pragmatism).

Naoko Saito is Associate Professor in the Graduate School of Education at Kyoto University, Japan. Her area of research is American philosophy and pragmatism and its implications for education. She is the author of *The Gleam of Light: Moral Perfectionism and Education in Dewey and Emerson* (2005).

INTRODUCTION

John Dewey's *Democracy and Education* in an Era of Globalization

This year marks the hundred-year anniversary of John Dewey's seminal work *Democracy and Education*. The centennial anniversary of Dewey's influential book presents philosophers and educators an opportunity to reexamine and evaluate its impact on various aspects of education in democratic societies. Thus, our goal in this special issue on John Dewey and education is to reflect on the legacy of *Democracy and Education* and, more generally, to consider the influence of Dewey's ideas on education in the twenty-first century. To be sure, a significant amount of books and articles have been published in the past several decades that address Dewey's views on education in general and on his conception of democratic education in particular. Our focus in this special issue, however, is to explore some important tensions and relationships among Dewey's ideas on democracy, education, and human flourishing in an era of globalization. Globalization is a contemporary phenomenon that has contributed to accelerated circulation of goods, information, and people around the globe. Globalization has played a significant role in the growing exposure of people to diverse histories, religions, and cultures; it has also contributed to the marginalization of workers and the displacement of many of our unifying principles such as neighborhoods and other local communities. Globalization has in many ways changed the shape of education by contributing to the marketization of education, the increase in digital technologies mediating interactions between teachers and students, and data-driven decision-making at all levels of education. These and other issues present us with new challenges to how we think about education. The contributors to this special issue attempt in various ways to make sense of how Dewey would have interpreted and responded to the phenomenon of globalization.

Some of the questions that we address in this issue on 'Dewey's *Democracy and Education* in an Era of Globalization' are as follows: To what extent was Dewey able to anticipate the changes and challenges to a democratic education that have been brought about by the phenomenon of globalization? What does a reexamination of Dewey's ideas on education bring to the current debate about the tensions between democracy and capitalism? How does his theory of democracy developed in *Democracy and Education* and other works advance our understanding of intercultural education? What insights can Dewey offer that could be relevant for the justification and continued development of philosophy for children in today's schools and classrooms? And finally, why after so many years might scholars and educators benefit by returning to Dewey for advice and insight? As we grapple with each of these questions, we seek to make new connections between theory and practice in education.

The first essay in this special issue is titled 'Globalization, Democracy, and Social Movements: The Educational Potential of Activism'. In this essay, Kathy Hytten explores the contemporary value of John Dewey's conception of democracy to addressing the challenges of neoliberal globalization. She begins by describing Dewey's vision of democracy as a way of life that requires habits of experimentalism, pluralism, and hope. Hytten then suggests that contemporary forms of mobilization, resistance, and insurgency—specifically alter-globalization activism, the Occupy Movement, and the Forward Together Moral Movement in North Carolina—model aspects of Deweyan democracy that are especially important for our times. These forms of civic activism can help reinvigorate Dewey's vision of democracy as rich, deep, participatory, and creative. Hytten argues that a significant value of these movements is the democratic habits and ways of life they encourage and support.

The next essay, authored by Jim Garrison, Stefan Neubert, and Kersten Reich, is titled 'Complexity and Reductionism in Educational Philosophy—John Dewey's Critical Approach in *Democracy and Education* Reconsidered'. Against the background of the Deweyan tradition of *Democracy and Education*, the authors discuss problems of complexity and reductionism in education and educational philosophy. The authors argue that powerful social tendencies of capitalist competition and social Darwinism support reductionisms in education and put the democratic project at risk. First, they investigate some of Dewey's own criticisms of reductionist tendencies in the educational traditions, theories, and practices of his time. Secondly, the authors explore some important cases of reductionism in the educational debates of our own day and argue that a similar criticism in behalf of democracy and education is appropriate and can easily be based on Deweyan terms. Thirdly, they draw some more general conclusions about complexity and reductionism as challenges for democracy and education. The authors show that the tensional relation between democracy and capitalism constitutes a major challenge for educational philosophy in our own time as much as in Dewey's.

In the third essay entitled, 'Not "democratic education" but "democracy and education": Reconsidering Dewey's oft Misunderstood Introduction to the Philosophy of Education', John Quay addresses the intimate connection Dewey draws between democracy and education in this seminal work. At first glance, Quay points out, the connection may appear quite simple, with the two terms commonly combined today as 'democratic education'. However, he argues that there is significantly more to Dewey's connection between democracy and education than 'democratic education' suggests. Quay illuminates some of the further riches Dewey offered to understanding democracy and education, central to which is his theorization of 'occupations' as this aligns with his attempts to articulate a 'coherent theory of experience'. As with democracy and education, the educational import of occupations cannot be captured with a mere combination of terms as in 'vocational education'. In both cases, we are simply appending an adjective to education, which Dewey found problematic. As Quay argues, an existential consideration of occupations enables us to realize that occupations include the functional unities of life, the character of social groupings, and the ways in which growth is arranged. As such, occupations provide us with new ways of conceptualizing the structure of schools and the nature of learning. Quay shows that in occupations, democracy and education come together in a much more fundamental sense as expressions of life.

Following this contribution is Megan Laverty's essay, '"Thinking my way back to you": John Dewey on Concept Formation'. In this essay, Laverty reexamines the chapters of Dewey's *Democracy and Education* that pertain to thinking and highlights their relationship to Dewey's work 'How We Think: A Restatement of the Relation of Reflective Thinking in the Educative Process'. In 'How We Think', Dewey explained that nothing is more important in education than the formation of concepts; they introduce permanency into an otherwise impermanent world. He defined concepts as established meanings, describing them as intellectual deposits used to fund a better understanding of new experiences. Concepts according to Dewey are what makes any experience educationally worthwhile. Dewey accused traditional and progressive education of failing to appropriately form concepts in students. Laverty shows that Dewey's position was that concepts are formed and transformed by experience, reflection, and activity. She concludes her essay with the practical recommendation that K-12 schools introduce philosophy into the curriculum. The introduction of philosophy in K-12 education would, Laverty suggests, offer a correction to both traditional and progressive education.

Andrea English's contribution to this special issue is titled 'John Dewey and the Role of the Teacher in a Globalized World: Imagination, Empathy and "Third Voice"'. English's discussion is situated in the context of current global higher education policy reforms surrounding the teacher's role in fostering students' social competences, especially those associated with empathy. These reforms—partly driven by the internationalization of higher education, which has brought diverse groups together within higher education learning environments—are calling for a shift away from lecture-style teaching, traditionally associated with higher education—toward student-centered teaching. English argues that these developments toward learner-oriented higher education teaching may offer promising opportunities—and, notably, they reference John Dewey's learning theory indicating his influence. However, English sees a central problem within these current policy recommendations in that the connection between cultivating *empathy* and cultivating *imagination* is not explicitly foregrounded. Drawing on Dewey's notion of imagination in learning, Martha Nussbaum's work on the narrative arts, and reflective examples from her own teaching experiences, English shows how cultivating students' imagination should be considered critical to the teacher's task. On this basis, English's paper provides significant insight into how Dewey's work can help philosophers, practitioners, and policy-makers to rethink what is needed to create inclusive classrooms in higher education, especially under conditions of cultural, linguistic, and religious diversity.

In 'American philosophy and its Eastern strains: Crisis, resilience, and self-transcendence', Naoko Saito critically reconsiders the potential of Dewey's pragmatist idea of *security without foundation*. She maintains that there is some potential in his antifoundationalism as a form of wisdom for living beyond the risk society. Saito argues that Deweyan critical thinking needs to be further reconstructed, and even destabilized, if it is to exercise its best possible power of transcendence. One way to do this is to open its boundaries toward the 'East', toward European poststructuralism as well as toward East Asia, thereby destabilizing and transcending the limits of pragmatism. Saito proposes to do this through the mediation of Stanley Cavell's rereading of Emerson's and Thoreau's American transcendentalism. Cavell's antifoundationalism can elucidate pragmatism's, and more broadly, American philosophy's *Eastern strains*, its troubled inheritance from Europe. Cavell's reinterpretation of American transcendentalism will reinforce American philosophy's antifoundationalism through the elaboration of a distinctive sense of transcendence—*transcendence in the ordinary.* This is a way of resisting the lure of foundationalism that today's global economy so easily proffers to us. Saito asserts that such critical reconstruction is necessary to make best use of the wisdom of Dewey's 'security without foundation.'

In the final essay of this special issue, 'Why should Scholars Keep Coming Back to John Dewey?' Mordechai Gordon attempts to explain why philosophers, philosophers of education, and scholars of democracy ought to keep coming back to John Dewey for insights and inspiration on issues related to democracy and education. Gordon proposes that there are at least four reasons that contribute to scholars' need to keep returning to Dewey. First, is Dewey's pragmatic educational approach that sought to maintain quality and stability in schools while rejecting the tendency to implement extreme changes in education based on the shifting winds of time. Second, is the fact that Dewey's works contain liberal and radical as well as modern and postmodern elements and, as such, it is difficult to label him as a member of one particular school of thought. Indeed, many of Dewey's essays and books can be viewed as a dialog between different ideological perspectives. Third, Dewey's body of research represents a wide range of topics and interests from art to politics and from philosophy to the nature and purpose of education. He provided thinkers with insights and food for thought on a variety of questions that are enduring in nature. However, Dewey's treatment of these diverse and complex topics is often dense and obscure, thereby opening up multiple avenues for interpretation. Finally, and perhaps most important, Gordon argues that Dewey's vision of democracy challenges us to recreate our global communities and our systems of education to meet the changing circumstances of history in such a way that all citizens can benefit. He called on the citizens of democratic societies to imagine new ways of association and interaction that promote a respect for freedom, equality, and diverse ways of being in the world.

MORDECHAI GORDON
School of Education, Quinnipiac University, Hamden, CT, USA
Mordechai.gordon@quinnipiac.edu

ANDREA R. ENGLISH
Institute for Education, Teaching and Leadership, Moray House School of Education, The University of Edinburgh, Edinburgh, UK
Andrea.english@ed.ac.uk

Globalization, Democracy, and Social Movements: The educational potential of activism

KATHY HYTTEN

Abstract

In this essay, I explore the contemporary value of John Dewey's conception of democracy to addressing the challenges of neoliberal globalization. I begin by describing his vision of democracy as a way of life that requires habits of experimentalism, pluralism, and hope. I then suggest that contemporary forms of mobilization, resistance, and insurgency—specifically, alter globalization activism, the Occupy Movement, and the Forward Together Moral Movement in North Carolina—model aspects of Deweyan democracy that are especially important for our times. These forms of civic activism can help reinvigorate Dewey's vision of democracy as rich, deep, participatory, and creative. I argue a significant value of these movements is the democratic habits and ways of life they encourage and support.

In reflecting on his book *Democracy and Education* in the late 1930s, John Dewey bemoaned the fact that we in the United States had come to see democracy as a static inheritance, rather than a dynamic process that required ongoing work and reinvention in each new generation. He was troubled by our seemingly insincere denouncement of others around the world (chastising the Nazis for cruelty, intolerance, and hatred), when at home we exhibited some of the same oppressive and violent behaviors, for example, through relentless segregation of, and hatred and prejudice toward, many of our own citizens. The denial of civil rights and mistreatment of African-Americans, Native Americans, women, and immigrants loomed large for Dewey, even as he didn't write about these issues as much as we might have assumed he would. He maintained that conflicts at home and abroad were in large part a problem of insufficient attention to the work of democracy. We had become complacent, acting as if 'democracy were something that perpetuated itself automatically ... as long as citizens were reasonably faithful in performing political duties,' presumably like voting and obeying laws (LW 14, 1939, p. 225). We had come to see democracy as a given, a gift bestowed on us by our forebears, rather than an experiment in living together that required ongoing work and nurturance.

Dewey's concerns about complacency resonate with our current realities. No doubt there are too many examples of citizen disengagement and passivity all around us. At the same time, enactments and performances of democracy around the world are often shallow. Voter turnout in elections is depressingly low, government decisions are increasingly shaped by corporate influence, income inequality is stark and growing, social support systems have eroded, and citizen apathy is often rampant. Green (2008) writes about dangerous habits of living that have become all too widespread in our contemporary era: 'constant busy-ness, fashionable cynicism, reliance on experts, willful ignorance of our nation's history and of current events, materialism, personal greed, and ... feelings of 'ontological insecurity,' generalized anxiety, and personal impotence' (p. 203). Yet at the same time, we see signs of hope for democratic renewal in growing social movements of diverse arrays of concerned citizens, from the alter globalization rallies in response to actions of international regulatory bodies such as the World Trade Organization, to Occupy Wall Street and its satellite occupations, from the Arab Spring and democratic protests around the world, to the contemporary Forward Together Moral Movement activism in the US South. Yet there is a real question as to which forces will shape our future. Can we create the deep, rich, participatory, and creative democracy that Dewey envisioned as the antidote to fundamentalism, totalitarianism, and elitist oligarchy? Or, will we continue to slide into cynicism and despair, fearing our fellow citizens, waging wars, distracting ourselves with vacuous entertainment, and hoarding individual resources, as we grow increasingly isolated from our neighbors and insecure about our futures?

In this paper, I argue that studying and participating in social movements can provide us with resources to help deepen democracy in the present. I focus in particular on progressive movements, that is, ones that center issues of social justice, equity, and diversity and call for expansive and inclusive notions of citizenship. These movements are rooted in Dewey's belief that 'what the best and wisest parent wants for his own child, that must the community want for all of its children' (MW 1, 1899, p. 5). Working to create the kind of rich, deep, participatory, and creative democracy that Dewey wrote about in *Democracy and Education* a century ago remains an important way to challenge disengaged cynicism and passivity in our present era. Dewey's vision of democracy is still timely; educating for democracy as a way of life and disposition toward others and the world is more necessary now than ever. At the same time, I suggest that contemporary forms of activism, mobilization, insurgency, and resistance are signs of hope that this deeper vision of democracy is both possible and increasingly desired by citizens from all walks of life. Rather than simply judge activist efforts for the concrete outcomes and changes they produce, we should see them as potential spaces for democratic renewal, where people can come together to learn and practice some of the most important habits of democratic citizenship, such as communication, cooperation, dialogue, experimentation, inquiry, empathy, solidarity, open-mindedness, and collective action. In working with others to speak back to injustice, and to create the conditions for all individuals to grow and thrive, we can begin to internalize the habits necessary to cultivate deep democracy.

JOHN DEWEY'S DEMOCRACY AND EDUCATION IN AN ERA OF GLOBALIZATION

Among the central themes of *Democracy and Education* is the critical role of education in preparing students for democratic citizenship. This entails both teaching so as to cultivate certain attitudes and dispositions, and helping students to envision a more desirable and just future and working to bring it into existence. It also involves seeing participation in social action and movements as forms of informal, yet nonetheless powerful, education. Education for democracy is precisely what we need today in order to speak back to the challenges of neoliberal, corporate-driven forms of globalization. That is, we need a complex and nuanced vision of democracy as a process where people see civic activism, informed by critical and collaborative inquiry, and an important habit of social engagement. Recent citizens' movements and protests can provide us with resources for cultivating and deepening the habits of democracy around the world. I argue that as educators, we should both habituate students for lives of civic engagement and activism and teach them about current movements and the possibilities they engender. Together, these actions push us closer toward realizing Dewey's vision of deep democracy as a way of everyday life.

I begin the first section of this essay by revisiting Dewey's vision for democracy and its relationship to education, something he most fully outlines in his now classic text, *Democracy and Education*. I illustrate how this vision is embedded in the work of several contemporary educational scholars attempting to create a more democratic foundation for education and schooling. Second, I identify some key Deweyan claims about democracy, focusing on the importance of habits of experimentalism, pluralism, and hope as integral features of a democratic way of life. I select these features in part because they are such important characteristics of contemporary social movements. Third, I describe the nature of several contemporary social movements and the potential ways in which they reflect a Deweyan vision of democracy, focusing particularly on alter globalization protests, the Occupy movement, and the Forward Together Moral Movement in North Carolina. Fourth, I read these movements through a Deweyan lens, arguing that they offer provocations for inquiry, new language for understanding social realities, and lessons for reinvigorating democracy in our times. They also provide opportunities for people to develop new tools for social change and to internalize important democratic habits, including empathy, solidarity, open-mindedness, responsibility, and collective action. I conclude by briefly discussing the educational implications of these movements, both how the movements themselves are educational to participants and witnesses, and how exploring these movements in schools can help students to see and understand a range of potentially transformative democratic possibilities. While I do not romanticize social movements, my ultimate claim is that they should provide us hope that Dewey's vision of deep democracy is indeed possible, and in nascent forms, already exists.

Dewey on Democracy

In one of his most well-known statements about democracy, Dewey writes that it 'is more than a form a government; it is primarily a mode of associated living, of conjoint, communicated experience' (MW 9, 1916, p. 93). He offers this description in chapter 7 of *Democracy and Education* after he has laid the groundwork for a progressive conception of education, where our central aim should be to cultivate the habits necessary for citizens to live together in ways that are peaceful, harmonious, individually enriching, and communally desirable. He argues that we need criteria, or a standard, to measure the quality of various modes of social life and to support why a democratic vision is indeed the most desirable. He is careful to point out that this vision of democracy must come from looking at the strengths of existing societies, not from some impractical or fanciful ideal. Most philosophers of education and democracy are familiar with the standard he offers: 'How numerous and varied are the interests which are consciously shared? How full and free is the interplay with other forms of association' (MW 9, 1916, p. 83)? This standard is both seductively simple and profound. He calls for us to seek out shared interests with others, eliminate barriers to communication across lines of difference, and develop common bonds, but at the same time to value a diversity of perspectives and interests and not to simply collapse these into a unified or homogeneous world view or social vision. In a democratic society, all voices are valued, institutions are flexible and change when they no longer meet peoples' needs, and citizens develop new habits when situations demand new forms of interaction.

Dewey rarely defines democracy in terms of systems or procedures, instead he wants us to first and foremost consider it a way of life. It is a way of life that is manifest when people hold certain attitudes and dispositions toward each other and the world. For example, they value inquiry and free communication, seek out multiple perspectives on information and phenomena, make decisions based upon the best evidence available, consider the impact of their choices on others both near and far, support and care about their fellow citizens, and work to develop shared interests. These dispositions are strengthened and reaffirmed within communities. Indeed, Dewey argues that idea of democracy is embedded in ideal community life, and that 'the clear consciousness of a communal life, in all its implications, constitutes the idea of democracy' (LW 2, 1927, p. 328). He writes that,

> Whenever there is conjoint activity whose consequences are appreciated as good by all singular persons who take part in it, and where the realization of the good is such as to effect an energetic desire and effort to sustain it in being just because it is a good shared by all, there is in so far a community. (LW 2, 1927, p. 328)

Here he implies that communities are democratic when they bring out the good in all of us, allow us to grow, and compel us to want others around us to grow as well.

For Dewey, democracy is a habit and way of being, more than a static inheritance or political system. It is a process that requires active engagement, not something we create and then institutionalize once and for all. It is a personal way of life and moral ideal that is premised on faith in our fellow citizens and their ability to use their minds well, act intelligently, make choices, construct goals, and assess the implications and consequences of potential actions. Describing this process, Dewey offers,

> Democracy is the faith that the process of experience is more important than any special result attained, so that special results achieved are of

> ultimate value only as they are used to enrich and order the ongoing process. Since the process of experience is capable of being educative, faith in democracy is all one with faith in experience and education. (LW 14, 1939, p. 229)

As he suggests, the foundation for this faith in the democratic process is education. Without schools that teach students the habits of inquiry and citizenship, we have no compelling reason to believe that people can or will work together, drawing on their experiences, in order 'to generate the aims and methods by which further experience will grow in ordered richness' (LW 14, 1939, p. 229).

We can see Deweyan democratic foundations in the work of a number of contemporary educators and scholars who are attempting to reinvigorate a democratic mission and vision for schools. These are important because they illustrate the Deweyan roots of contemporary approaches to democratic education, and because they translate his sometimes-abstract philosophical ideas into concrete strategies and practices that can be enacted in schools today. For example, Beane and Apple (2007) argue that democracy ought to be the benchmark, standard, and ethical anchor that we use to assess with 'wisdom and worth' of our social policies, educational practices, and international relationships (p. 5). Drawing from Dewey, they describe democracy as an ongoing endeavor whose moral heart entails upholding the dignity and worth of individuals while they work together to achieve common goods. Indeed, the values and principles that Beane and Apple outline for democratic schools make concrete some of Dewey's more abstract philosophical ideals. For example, democratic schools teach students, as citizens in the making, to value the rights and dignities of all people, including and especially those historically marginalized; care about diverse others and common goods; cherish an open flow of ideas, even when some are unpopular; use skills of critical analysis and reflection to evaluate problems and ideas; maintain faith in the capacity of individuals and groups to understand and resolve problems; draw on democratic ideals to ground their life choices; and organize and promote systems, policies, and institutions that support and further a democratic way of life (p. 7).

Similarly, Ayers, Kumashiro, Meiners, Quinn, and Stovall (2010) also trace their understanding of democracy as an 'aspiration to be continuously nourished, engaged, and exercised' (p. 14) with each new generation to Deweyan roots. They too argue we must educate students so that they internalize democratic values, learning to question, dialog, critique, imagine, create, and change their worlds. They offer a vision of democracy built on the same fragile ideal that Dewey described: that all individuals, regardless of race, class, gender, and belief systems, are

> ... of infinite and incalculable value, each a unique intellectual, emotional, physical, spiritual, moral, and creative force, each born free and equal in dignity and rights, endowed with reason and conscience, and deserving, then, a community of solidarity, a sense of brotherhood and sisterhood, recognition and respect. (p. 12)

These democratic visions for schooling have been significantly muted in our current educational climate where standardization, competition, and narrowly defined forms of academic achievement are celebrated above all else. Moreover, information regurgitation is substituted for inquiry, job preparation is thought to be more important than teaching students how to make a meaningful life, and student worth is often reduced to their scores on standardized tests. This is hardly the vision Dewey had for education in, and for, democracy.

Habits of Democracy

As a process, democracy entails ongoing work and vigilance. It requires that we cultivate habits of engaging the world that allow us to address timely challenges and chart new possibilities for individual and communal growth. Dewey often spoke about democracy in the language of habits. In contrast to the narrow, and generally more familiar, view of habits as behaviors we engage in thoughtlessly and routinely, like brushing our teeth in the morning, he held a more complex view of the meaning and importance of habits. Stitzlein (2014) describes his perspective well. She writes, 'for Dewey, habit should be understood as a predisposition to act, or sensitivity to ways of being—rather than the more common understanding of habit as an inclination to repeat identical acts or address content precisely' (p. 63). We adopt habits as part of everyday living, through implicit and explicit lessons we learn from our families, interactions with members of our communities, media and popular culture, and the organizations and institutions of which we are a part. While habits are acquired in all social settings, 'their cultivation is often most overt in schools, where children watch, imitate, and interact with others as they learn about socially acceptable behaviors and societal traditions, through both direct and indirect means' (Stitzlein, 2014, p. 65). While we sometimes teach students directly how to behave and interact, for example, through character education programs, most habits are learned and developed more unconsciously, through implicitly adopting ways of being that are conducive to success in schools. This is why the environments we create in schools are so important. Among a range of possibilities, we have the potential to shape students into critical, democratic thinkers, or disengaged, passive followers who implicitly seek to uphold the status quo, rather than challenge it in the interests of equity and justice.

Among the most important habits of democracy that Dewey advocated for, and that are especially relevant to reflection on social activism, are experimentalism, pluralism, and hope. The idea of experimentalism is at the heart of Dewey's conception of democracy. As a pragmatist, he thought we should engage the world around us critically, always seeking better, more enriching, ways of living and working together. Moreover, we should regularly question prevailing ideas, practices, and policies and assess them in terms of how well they work in practice. When our practices no longer achieve our desired goals, or when ours ways of doing things have stagnated, we should experiment with new possibilities. Specifically, we should identify problems, explore their causes, hypothesize about possible solutions, reason about ways for testing our solutions, and then try out the most promising possibilities. This experimentalist habit is part and parcel of democratic living. Dewey wrote that a society which ensures equal participation in social life for all its members 'and which secures flexible readjustment of its institutions through interaction of the different forms of associated life is in so far democratic' (MW 9, 1916, p. 105). The habit of experimentalism applies to both reflecting on existing institutions and to creating collaborative possibilities, for example, in the kinds of new alliances, coalitions, and communities developed through social movements and activism.

Pluralism goes hand-in-hand with experimentalism, in large part because a range of different ways of thinking and doing is a prerequisite to imagining and trying out alternative possibilities. Considering pluralism as a habit means we are compelled regularly to seek out new people and perspectives and to search for commonalities even while we attempt to understand and value differences. Dewey prized 'diversity of stimulation,' because it leads to 'novelty, and novelty means challenge to thought,' and it is through challenges that we grow (MW 9, 1916, p. 90). He maintained that we need to hear many different voices and perspectives in order to generate ideas and tools to best confront our most pressing social problems. Moreover, our individual lives are enriched the more we surround ourselves with people who see the world differently from us, and who bring different resources to our collaborative endeavors. Describing the importance of pluralistic communities in Dewey's work, Kurth-Schai (2014) writes that, 'diversity, as an enduring source of imagination and innovation, provides the basis of continuing experimentation and growth' (p. 429). Seeking out and experimenting with new ideas and possibilities, and making connections across perspectives, help us to strengthen our commitments to our fellow citizens.

Experimentalism and pluralism are characteristic features of much contemporary social activism. Social and economic change movements that most model a Deweyan vision are not typically driven by a single ideology, but by people from all walks of life working in a variety of disparate contexts. Sometimes they interact in more homogeneous groups and sometimes they engage side-by-side with people who hold different passions and agendas, yet who are also working to create a more just, humane, and peaceful future. In fact, a distinctive feature of many contemporary forms of social justice activism are their diversity of goals: civil rights, indigenous sovereignty, clean water, protection of public goods, affordable and nutritious food, access to health care, people before profits, security, peace, environmental protection, sustainable energy, education, economic justice, etc. Describing this growing progressive and diverse social movement, Hawken (2007) offers, 'if the movement in all its diversity has a common dream, it is process—in a word, democracy, but not the democracy practiced and corrupted by corporations and modern-nation states' (p. 18). Rather, it is democracy as the way of life that Dewey imagined, where ordinary citizens speak back to oppressive power in myriad ways, gaining strength from 'autonomy within diversity,' and by creating the conditions through which 'groups with varying outlooks and discrete goals cooperate on key issues without subordinating themselves to another group' (Hawken, 2007, p. 18). Through working with others on issues that they are passionate about, citizens ideally develop the habits of experimentalism and pluralism, as well as the habit of hope, sustained by evidence that other worlds are possible. In fact, the relationships and communities developed within social movements bring these other worlds into existence.

As a disposition and habit of being, hope entails action. It requires that we imagine possibilities and work to help them emerge. Solnit (2006) describes hope as an orientation of the soul, spirit, and heart that is sustained when we work with others to cultivate the good (p. 149). A habit of hope is sustained by pragmatic meliorism, or the belief that through critical thinking and experimental action, we can bring about better worlds. Despite the many evils and tragedies humanity has to contend with, Deweyan pragmatists believe that 'there are always experientially warranted distinctions to be made between the worse and the better—in hypotheses and beliefs, in historical interpretations, in values, in words, in public policies, in actions, and in life choices' (Green, 2008, p. 245). That is, choosing to act on the better, after careful consideration of various options, matters. There is no certainty that our actions will have the desired effects, but we should act as if they could, and learn and grow from what happens in response to our actions and choices. This can allow us to then 'more effectively recognize and achieve 'the better' on future occasions' (Green, 2008, p. 245).

In social movements, activists talk about the habit of hopefulness in terms of the 'politics of prefiguration,' by which they mean that when we live out the values we are working for in our relationships with others, and in our communities, then those values have already become a way of life. Solnit (2006) writes that 'if your activism is already democratic, peaceful, creative, then in one small corner of the world these things have triumphed' (p. 87). These victories then become inspiration for future actions, and for creating more experimental, pluralistic, and hopeful possibilities. These Deweyan habits are often enacted in contemporary social movement activism, especially when participants are reflective about the strengths and limitations of their visions, strategies, and action. Reading these movements through a Deweyan lens can help us to reinvigorate his vision of deep, participatory democracy, as well as to ensure that the habit of hope becomes more widespread in our world, muting the competing forces of cynicism and despair.

Contemporary Social Movements

It is challenging to succinctly capture the potentially democratic nature of social activism, especially present in movements that are the most Deweyan in spirit. Arguably, social movements fall on a range from more conservative (e.g. tea-party activism, pro-life or fundamentalist rallies) to more progressive (coalitions of diverse people working together to ensure greater equality of opportunity, access, and life outcomes for all citizens, such as the examples I describe in this essay). Certainly habits of civic engagement can be cultivated in any type of social movement, even ones that on the surface seem to truncate rather than enrich the development and expansion of democracy, seek to limit the rights and agency of marginalized individuals rather than extending them, and fail to be inclusive of multiple voices and perspectives. Yet, Dewey's work provides us some ideals and criteria from which to assess the democratic potential of all social movements. For example, we ought to explore the degree to which movement participants value inquiry, diversity, and inclusion, while creating spaces 'for participation in its good of all its members on equal terms' (Dewey, MW 9, 1916, p. 105) and adjusting operating processes, procedures, and goals based on the interactions among these diverse groups. Moreover, when they are at their most democratic, social movements help us to balance individual desires with commitment to common goods, and to live together in ways where 'the life of each of us is at once profitable in the deepest sense of the word, profitable to himself and helpful in the building up of the individuality of others' (Dewey, LW 13, 1938, p. 303).

From civil rights movements, to anti-war protests, to rallies against government oppression around the world, citizens have always resisted oppressive power and sought to create different worlds. The contemporary era of neoliberal globalization has sparked a new wave of unrest around the world, marked in part by coalitions of workers, students, and activists taking to the streets to call attention to abusive government power and corporate greed. While contemporary social movements are often similar to those that have occurred in the past, there is something unique also about their global scope and the new forms of activism enabled by technological advancements. Solnit (2006) marks the symbolic beginning of this new era of civic action and protest with the fall of the Berlin wall in 1989 and the consequent end of cold war politics and isolation. She then highlights several other emblematic moments of growing civic activism: the Zapatista revolt in Mexico in 1994 on the day the North American Free Trade Agreement went into effect, the shutting down of the World Trade Organization meetings in Seattle in 1999, and the worldwide protests against the invasion of Iraq in 2003.

Since the dawn of the twenty-first century, we have witnessed numerous other protests, small and large, aiming to alter the course of neoliberal globalization. We can see these as part of a global justice movement that challenges the seemingly unrestricted power of multinational corporations to elevate profits above worker rights, environmental protections, and national sovereignty. We have also witnessed large-scale citizens movements against oppressive governments, in Thailand in 2010, Iran in 2011, and all over the Arab world between late 2010 and 2012 in what has become known as the Arab Spring. Protesters in these movements were speaking back against many issues, including government repression, corruption, and secrecy; fundamentalist oligarchy; widespread poverty; growing income gaps; and human and civil rights abuses. They were implicitly and explicitly advocating for more democratic social, economic, and political arrangements, that is, spaces where we are committed to the well-being of all, not the aggrandizement or profiteering of a few.

More recently, the Occupy movement captured the public imagination. It began in September of 2011, when a group of about 1000 activists set up encampments at a public park along Wall Street in New York City, a symbolic hub of corporate greed. Asserting themselves as the 99% who don't hold the majority of the world's wealth, the protestors claimed space (maintaining encampments for months) as a way to criticize 'the growth of social inequalities and the rising influence of corporate companies and lobbyists on the US government' (Kern & Nam, 2013, p. 196). This 'leaderless, people-powered resistance movement' (Catalano, 2013, p. 276) spread to numerous locations worldwide as the idea of 'occupying' public space became a visual representation of a growing desire among many for a more responsive and representative democracy. Loosely united by a quest for greater income equality, like the alter globalization activists before them, occupiers held a myriad of passions and goals, from human rights, to environmental justice, to universal health care and greater protection for workers. While criticized for not having specific and unified demands, occupiers succeeded in transforming the notion of 'occupation' itself. Where it historically referred to an ongoing military takeover, many now see it as a powerful ideal that 'signifies standing up to injustice, inequality and abuse of power. It's no longer simply about occupying a space; it is about transforming that space' (Alim, 2011).

In a very general sense, the end goal of occupying is to create more democratic social and economic relations in and through our actions. Occupying is symbolic; it represents people claiming space as citizens, in part to ensure issues of oppression and justice are a central part of our public discourse. In fact, Ruggerio (2012) suggests, 'that one of the movement's greatest successes has been to put the inequalities of everyday life on the national agenda, influencing reporting, public awareness and language itself' (p. 9). For example, no doubt the Occupy movement made the language of the '99% versus the 1%' a way of making sense of social realities that deeply resonates with many people. Moreover, arguably we are now talking about issues of economic and social inequality in the mass media more than we have in a long time in this country. It is only when we are aware of the myriad dimensions of social injustice, and know the contours of prevailing social and economic problems, that we can experiment with ways of creating more democratic possibilities.

Even more recently, the Forward Together Moral Movement took off in North Carolina in 2013. After years of fairly progressive politics, ultraconservative Republicans took over both the legislature (in 2010) and the governor's office (in 2012) and began instituting some of the most regressive policies ever seen in the state, including cutting education funding, reducing unemployment benefits and Medicaid coverage, slashing taxes for the wealthy and raising them for the bottom 95%, limiting a woman's right to make decisions about her body, and restricting voting rights (Berman, 2013). Though the seeds had been laid for many years, the movement started in earnest with a rally on Jones Street in Raleigh in February of 2013 that brought together a diverse array of people seeking more social, economic, and political justice.

From the start, those involved in the Forward Together Moral Movement sought to create inclusive alliances, advocating for five broad, 'nonpartisan' human values: economic sustainability and an end to poverty, educational equality, universal health care, fairness in the criminal justice system, and voting rights (Barber, 2014, p. 12). This rally was followed by weekly rallies, 'Moral Mondays,' on the steps of the North Carolina Senate and House that steadily grew in size. Next were satellite rallies around the state, grassroots mobilizations, voter registration drives, and educational campaigns, culminating in the Moral March on Raleigh in February of 2014. Estimates of upwards of 80,000 people attended this March, making it 'the largest civil rights rally in the South since the legendary Selma-to-Montgomery march in support of the Voting Rights Act in 1965' (Berman, 2014, p. 23). Among the most powerful features of the Forward Together Moral Movement is what the movement's 'most visible leader,' Reverend William Barber II, calls a 'transformative fusion coalition.' He explains, 'transformative fusion means that each organization came to the coalition with a deep commitment not just to advance their own political priorities ... but to advance the various causes of the other coalition members as well' (McLain, 2014,

p. 24). This diverse, multi-issue movement is a powerful example of a Deweyan approach to participatory democracy, one that illustrates the importance of experimental, pluralistic, and hopeful collaborative and visionary action to create new worlds. Ultimately, what joins together the alter globalization, Occupy, and Forward Together movements is when they are at their best, modeling ideals that are always hard to achieve practice, they reflect Deweyan visions for inclusive and progressive democracy.

Civic Activism and Deweyan Deep Democracy

Viewing contemporary social movements like alter globalization, Occupy, and the Forward Together Moral Movement through a Deweyan lens, we can see them as examples of experimental projects that in some ways model his democratic criteria: shared points of connection, along with free and flexible interactions between groups that hold different goals. They are also offer examples of how Green (2008) describes democracy as an active, participatory, and engaged way of life, in contrast with the more common 'representative' forms of democracy that are typically experienced as distant from individual passions and concerns. Within social movements, participants can learn habits of interaction, compromise, collaboration, and collective action. Ideally, they come to adopt what Dewey described as democracy as a personal way of life. They learn to rely on their own and their 'fellow citizens' developable capacities for cooperative self-government' in order to resist the 'very real antidemocratic forces' that surround them while working to create meaningful local and global partnerships for justice (Green, 2008, p. 234). Green (2008) suggests that alter globalization movements, and the kinds of large-scale civic actions they inspire, are so valuable because they help to instill democratic habits and dispositions. They teach respect and shared responsibility, support the development of cooperative solutions to problems, break down ignorance-based barriers between groups, disperse local knowledges, cultivate the practical intelligence of participants, and honor individual gifts. She adds that on the ground, activist, participatory democracy is 'redemptive because it encourages the democratic spirit in individuals; it builds community, while encouraging values like compassion, tolerance, and equality; and it transforms institutions to make them more effective instruments of democracy' (Green, 2008, p. 241). In the disruption of the status quo and the restlessness for ways of living that are more meaningful and fulfilling, at their best, contemporary social movements are a hopeful manifestation of participatory democracy in action.

Civic activism, in the form of organizing, marching, rallying, protesting, and occupying, contributes to creating the habits of democracy in two important ways. First, movements help participants to learn skills for organizing, communicating, and sharing ideas. Solnit (2006) claims that they create 'a vocabulary and a toolbox for social change,' that has ripple effects that far outweigh the successes of any particular movement (p. 61). Second, acting to bring about the good, however partial and flawed the outcomes of our efforts, helps us to internalize important democratic habits and values. Through engaging with others to create meaningful change, we learn to see democracy as a way of life that requires our ongoing attention, rather than becoming cynical and complacent in the face of antidemocratic forces. Being around other justice-oriented people, seeking common causes and developing shared passions, is energizing and educational, especially when inquiry is valued alongside advocacy, and when participants teach and learn together about the historic roots of contemporary problems. Working with others on overlapping goals, we learn how to listen, cooperate, compromise, and communicate. Among the most distinctive features of the alter globalization and Occupy movements are the use of horizontal forms of decision-making and consensus building through affinity groups, general assemblies, and spokes-council meetings. Movement participants create broadly inclusive communities and educate each other as central parts of spreading movement ideas and visions.

Describing the educative process and potential in relation to the Occupy Movement, Rushkoff (2013) argues that the approach of the occupiers was 'more like a university' than typical social movements or protests of the past. That is, they represent new ways of speaking back to power. Both face-to-face settings and online forums are comprised largely of 'teach-ins' about shared concerns and how to best educate others. He describes how 'young people teach one another or invite guests to lecture them about subjects such as how the economy works, the disconnection of investment banking from the economy of goods and services ... and even best practices for civil disobedience' (p. 171). Similarly, Chomsky (2012) suggests that one of the most remarkable features of Occupy was the creation of cooperative communities, 'that include general assemblies that carry out extensive discussion, kitchens, libraries, support systems and so on' (p. 57). These are models for new community structures that could be spread into other contexts. At the same time, within these emergent communities, individuals learn leadership skills, problem-solving, political strategies, and how to craft accessible messages to the broader public. These 'tactics and practices devised by activists become part of a collective political know-how, a political jurisprudence of sorts that functions as a toolbox available for anyone else to use' (Arditi, 2015, p. 135). Most importantly, movement participants embody the belief that democracy is an ongoing process that requires citizen participation, voice, and action.

While learning new skills and tools, and developing collaborative communities, movement participants also ideally come to internalize new attitudes, habits, and dispositions. This is perhaps the strongest democratic potential of social movements. In the gathering of thoughtful, critical, justice-minded citizens, people can learn the values of experimentalism, pluralism, and hope. They can also learn that process is as important as outcomes, and that diverse, multifaceted, developmental approaches to social change have the greatest potential to alter our world, not simply one-shot marches and/or symbolic rallies. Indeed, one of the distinctive features of the new wave of social activism, including alter globalization protests, Occupy, and the Forward Together Moral Movement, are that they are ongoing movements, not moments. They aim to transform ways of seeing and fundamental values and to create visions for new worlds. They offer new vocabulary and ways of being in relation to each other and to the world. Arditi (2015) argues that such insurgencies open up new possibilities, and through 'challenging our political imaginaries and cognitive maps ... [they] are passageways between worlds. They are a way of enacting the promise of something other to come' (p. 116).

We can see the Deweyan potential of progressive movement activism most strongly in the Forward Together Moral Movement, especially in the coalitional approach and the ways in which the movement inspired inquiry surrounding intersectional nature of social problems. After multiple years of strategic actions in North Carolina that provided the foundation for the weekly Moral Mondays, the organizers of the Forward Together Moral Movement learned a number of lessons on social movement building that are relevant to creating new democratic habits and expectations. For movements to instill such democratic habits, participants must 'engage in indigenously led grassroots organizing', use moral language to frame issues; create spaces for all voices, not a stage for partisan politics; consciously 'diversify the movement with the goal of winning unlikely allies', build long-term, transformative coalitions; use social media of all forms to spread messages and build communities; make a commitment to academic and empirical analyses; and resist a 'one moment mentality' in favor of movement building (Barber, 2014, pp. 161–162). All of these strategies resonate with Dewey's vision of democracy as a lived, participatory process, one where inquiry and collaborative problem-solving are valued, not simply conspicuous forms of public action and protest.

One of the more powerful aspects of the Forward Together Moral Movement is the ways in which organizers and participants have identified a number of shared interests and a 'people's agenda' for the future of the state that begins with a commitment to 'high quality, constitutional, well-funded, diverse public schools' (HKonJ People's Assembly Coalition, n.d.). The research-based, 14-point agenda brings together a range of important social issues, from creating living wages, to providing health care for all citizens, fixing regressive election policies, and redressing historic forms of discrimination. The movement works on multiple fronts, providing many spaces for citizens to get involved, both in their local communities and as part of larger gatherings. Like alter globalization and Occupy, the Forward Together Moral Movement reflects what Dewey argues is the 'task of democracy,' which 'is forever that of creation of a freer and more humane experience in which all share and to which all contribute' (LW 14, 1939, p. 230).

Ultimately, when they are at their best, meaning they balance advocacy with education and inquiry, and work to identify broad goals and action plans for achieving them, contemporary social movements ought to provide us with a sense of hope that other, healthier, more enriching, ways of living together are possible. Activists don't have 'the' answer to cultivating the participatory and individually affirming democracy that Dewey envisioned. Instead, they offer us multiple possible answers and visions that can fuel what ought to be our restless efforts to create better worlds. At the very least, they show that we can imagine and work toward more humane and just social, political, and economic relations throughout the world.

Final Thoughts on the Educational Potential of Activism

I have argued throughout this essay that contemporary progressive social movements, rooted in social justice visions of equity and human flourishing, often embody the spirit of Deweyan democracy and can provide inspiration for reinvigorating democracy in the present. I don't want to romanticize these movements, however. They are sometimes chaotic and unfocused, and are often short on practical strategies for creating lasting political or institutional changes. They sometimes encourage participants to support stances narrowly and reductively, resulting in a kind of ardent close-mindedness that can inhibit the spirit of Deweyan inquiry. This is especially the case when complex positions get reduced to slogans on bumper stickers or protest signs. Moreover, progressive movements are not inherently more democratic than conservative movements, even as the expressed ideals that they work towards are generally more consistent with Dewey's vision of democracy than, for example, the goals of members of conservative groups who (however consciously) seek to maintain the privileges of the already-privileged (e.g. by opposing affirmative action, immigration, language diversity, national health care, and social services). Social movements are also fleeting, even as the 'longing that gives rise to these movements, the relationships they shape, and the special skills they develop usually continue to seek new transformative outlets' (Green, 2008, p. 191). Yet we should also not underestimate their potential, especially as forces for democratic learning and renewal. The movements themselves can be educational, especially when they involve teach-ins, information sharing, the linking of theory and practice, and the translation of ideas into accessible visions and strategic actions. Participants learn skills, habits, and tools for social change that they can bring back to their own local communities. Ideally, they also learn about social issues, how to research these issues, and about the historically rooted interconnections among various forms of oppression and struggle. Movements provide laboratories for trying out new political strategies and tactics, and for building alliances and coalitions.

To enhance their potential impact and power, we should teach about ongoing social movements in schools, in part to ensure students as 'citizens in the making' develop democratic dispositions and habits. Teaching more about these movements in schools can help students to embrace the idea of democracy as an active way of life, rather than a static inheritance. It can also help to dispel the notion that the outcomes of movements are inherently more important than their processes and the habits we can develop when we work with others on important social issues. One of the points of democratic activism is to grow along with others, to be most fully alive as we transform our worlds in ways that both support individual enrichment and sustain common goods. Participation in movements, large and small, allows 'us to glimpse something other to come…to experience what…[we] strive to become' (Arditi, 2015, p. 113). At its best, such participation supports habits of questioning, inquiry, engagement, compassion, collaboration, compromise, and hope. It keeps social injustice on the national agenda, along with visions of more genuinely democratic forms of association.

One of Dewey's most enduring lessons is about the fragility of democracy. Among its greatest threats are passivity, complacency, and hopelessness. At their best, social movements like those that I have described in this essay inspire hope, and provide spaces for democratic aspirations and dreams to be lived out. Along with schools, they offer an avenue to learn some of the most important habits of democracy: citizenship as shared fate, collaboration and compromise, deliberation, analysis and critique, and hope (Stitzlein, 2014). They provide opportunities for growth and connection, and for existential meaning. Discussing the attraction of participating in social movements, Green (2008) asserts that it is not a sense of 'purity or infinitude but a meaningful life and one's own better becoming through participating in a shared, transgenerationally effective agency in shaping a world that reflects our ideals' (p. 191). This is the kind of life Dewey imagined, one that brings out the best in each of us as we work to create the conditions for all to grow and thrive.

In the end, the broad goal of many progressive forms of social activism is to engage with others in critiquing social injustice and oppression, imagining new worlds, and working to bring them into existence. Even as we might not always achieve the short or long-term goals we imagine, it is only in the process of working for the better that we can actually create the better. For Dewey, this was a world where all individuals could reach their full potential and where we want for other people's children the same things we want for our own children. Contemporary social movements, in all of their diversity and richness, and along with all their flaws, are signs of hope that the deep, rich, participatory democracy that Dewey envisioned is indeed possible, and in fleeting moments, already exists.

Disclosure statement

No potential conflict of interest was reported by the author.

References

Alim, S. (2011). What if we occupied language? *New York Times*, December 21. http://opiniona tor.blogs.nytimes.com/2011/12/21/what-if-we-occupied-language/?_r=0

Arditi, B. (2015). Insurgencies don't have a plan—they *are* the plan. In C. de la Torre (Ed.), *Power to the people? The promise and perils of populism* (pp. 113–139). Lexington, KY: University of Kentucky Press.

Ayers, W., Kumashiro, K., Meiners, E., Quinn, T., & Stovall, D. (2010). *Teaching toward Democracy: Educators as agents of change*. Boulder, CO: Paradigm Publishers.

Barber, W. J. (2014). *Forward together: A moral message for the nation*. St. Louis, MO: Chalice Press.

Beane, J. A. & Apple, M. W. (2007). The case for democratic schools. In M. W. Apple & J. A. Beane (Eds.), *Democratic schools: Lessons in powerful education* (2nd ed.). (pp. 1–29). Portsmouth, NH: Heinemann.

Berman, A. (2013, August 5/12). Carolina's moral Mondays. *The Nation, 297*, 8–9.

Berman, A. (2014, March 10/17). What's next for the moral Monday movement? *The Nation, 298*, 23–25.

Catalano, T. (2013). Occupy: A case illustration of social movements in global citizenship education. *Education, Citizenship and Social Justice, 8*, 276–288.

Chomsky, N. (2012). *Occupy*. Brooklyn, NY: Occupied Media Pamphlet Series, Zuccotti Park Press.

Dewey, J. (1899). School and society. In J. A. Boydston (Ed., 1976), *John Dewey: The middle works, 1899–1924* (Vol. 1, pp. 1–112). Carbondale, IL: Southern Illinois University Press. Referred to as MW 1.

Dewey, J. (1916). Democracy and education. In J. A. Boydston (Ed., 1980), *John Dewey: The middle works, 1899–1924* (Vol. 9, pp. 4–384). Carbondale, IL: Southern Illinois University Press. Referred to as MW 9.

Dewey, J. (1927). The public and its problems. J. A. Boydston (Ed., 1984), *John Dewey: The later works, 1925–1953* (Vol. 2, pp. 235–372). Carbondale, IL: Southern Illinois University Press. Referred to as LW 2.

Dewey, J. (1938). Democracy and education in the world of today. In J. A. Boydston (Ed., 2008), *John Dewey: The later works, 1925–1953* (Vol. 13, pp. 294–303). Carbondale, IL: Southern Illinois University Press. Referred to as LW 13.

Dewey, J. (1939). Creative democracy—the task before us. In J. A. Boydston (Ed., 2008), *John Dewey: The later works, 1925–1953* (Vol. 14, pp. 224–230). Carbondale, IL: Southern Illinois University Press. Referred to as LW 14.

Green, J. M. (2008). *Pragmatism and social hope: Deepening democracy in global contexts*. New York, NY: Columbia University Press.

Hawken, P. (2007). *Blessed unrest: How the largest social movement in history is restoring grace, justice, and beauty to the world*. New York, NY: Penguin Books.

HKonJ People's Assembly Coalition. (n.d.). 14 Point People's Agenda for North Carolina. http://www.hkonj.com/14_point_agenda.

Kern, T., & Nam, S. (2013). From 'corruption' to 'democracy': Cultural values, mobilization, and the collective identity of the occupy movement. *Journal of Civil Society, 9*, 196–211.

Kurth-Schai, R. (2014). Fidelity in public education policy: Reclaiming the Deweyan dream. *Educational Studies, 50*, 420–446.

McLain, D. (2014, July 21/28). Moral Mondays and the 'fusion coalition'. *The Nation, 299*, 23–25.

Ruggerio, G. (2012). Editors note. In N. Chomsky (Ed.), *Occupy* (pp. 9–19). Brooklyn, NY: Occupied Media Pamphlet Series, Zuccotti Park Press.

Rushkoff, D. (2013). Permanent revolution: Occupying democracy. *The Sociological Quarterly, 54*, 159–228.

Solnit, R. (2006). *Hope in the dark: Untold histories, wild possibilities*. New York, NY: Nation Books.

Stitzlein, S. (2014). Habits of Democracy: A Deweyan approach to citizenship education in America today. *Education and Culture, 30*, 61–86.

Complexity and Reductionism in Educational Philosophy—John Dewey's Critical Approach in 'Democracy and Education' Reconsidered

KERSTEN REICH, JIM GARRISON & STEFAN NEUBERT

Abstract

Against the background of the Deweyan tradition of Democracy and Education, *we discuss problems of complexity and reductionism in education and educational philosophy. First, we investigate some of Dewey's own criticisms of reductionist tendencies in the educational traditions, theories, and practices of his time. Secondly, we explore some important cases of reductionism in the educational debates of our own day and argue that a similar criticism in behalf of democracy and education is appropriate and can easily be based on Deweyan terms. Thirdly, we draw some more general conclusions about complexity and reductionism as challenges for democracy and education. Among other things, we argue that powerful social tendencies of capitalist competition and social Darwinism support reductionisms in education and put the democratic project at risk. The tensional relation between democracy and capitalism constitutes a major challenge for educational philosophy in our own time as much as in Dewey's.*

1. Introduction

In this essay, we intend to proceed in three steps: First, we will argue that Dewey's approach to democracy and education that so influenced twentieth century educational philosophy was based on several critical responses to serious reductionisms in the educational traditions of his time. We will show that his criticisms of classical approaches, like Rousseau, Herbart, Froebel and also Plato and Hegel, serve not only as a background but also as a constructive medium for the generation of his own positions. The main targets of his criticisms are several versions of philosophical reductionisms that have to do with experience, the world of action, the construction of communities, and the like. His fundamental philosophical insights about the necessity of context and the need to avoid one-sided intellectualism constitute the basis for these critical accounts. Second, we then go on to focus on several important and influential reductionisms in the educational discourses and practices since Dewey's lifetime and argue that a similar employment of criticism as a constructive medium for the generation of a sufficiently comprehensive and contextualized approach to democracy and education is necessary in our time. We will deal, for example, with the notorious influence of reductionist behaviorism and narrow conceptualizations of learning in twentieth century education. The main target of these criticisms are several versions of instrumental reductionism in education, the social sciences, and psychology that have to do with experience, learning, teaching, communication, and the like. Finally, we briefly summarize what we think are lessons to be learned and necessary implications of these critical and constructive movements for the future of democracy and education. Among other things, our focus will be on connecting Deweyan education with essential claims and challenges in our time.

2. Dewey's Criticism of Reductionist Approaches in Education

Seen from today's perspective Dewey appears as a twentieth century philosopher who expresses a unique sensitivity to the importance of contexts and an acute awareness for the need to avoid reductionism and to criticize all of its forms. For instance, unlike many of his contemporary admirers of modernization, Dewey strongly rejects scientism and positivism.

In several chapters of *Democracy and Education* Dewey criticizes selected philosophical traditions in education, especially with regard to their implicit reductionism. He does so in an exemplary way to prepare the grounds for his own positive approach to experience and education that considers reductionisms of all sorts and provides theoretical and conceptual instruments for deconstructing their claims and limits. Among others, he chooses traditions from Plato, Locke, Rousseau, Kant, Pestalozzi, Froebel, Herbart, Fichte, and Hegel. We confine ourselves here to briefly addressing his criticisms of Plato, Rousseau, Froebel, Herbart, and Hegel.

Dewey takes Plato as an influential tradition regarding the social import of education in connection with 'democratic ideas in education' (MW 9, p. 94). He declares:

> No one could better express than did he the fact that a society is stably organized when each individual is doing that for which he has aptitude by nature in such a way as to be useful to others (or to contribute to the whole to which he belongs); and that it is the business of education to discover these aptitudes and progressively to train them for social use. (MW 9, p. 94)

Dewey agrees we must understand education and social organization as interconnected. However, he readily identifies Plato's major shortcoming: 'He never got any conception of the indefinite plurality of activities which may characterize an individual and a social group, and consequently limited his view to a limited number of classes of capacities and of social arrangements' (MW 9, p. 94). Plato assumes we must have knowledge in advance of the ends of existence; otherwise 'we shall have no criterion for rationally deciding what the possibilities are which should be promoted, nor how social arrangements are to be ordered' (MW 9, p. 94). Plato envisioned a static hierarchical society in which 'few men, philosophers or lovers of wisdom—or truth—may by study learn at least in outline the proper patterns of true existence' (MW 9, p. 95). The task of education was to sift the populous into three perpetually fixed classes (warriors, artisans, and philosopher kings). Plato assumed a meritocracy where individuals came to occupy their social position not by birth, but by ability. While Dewey prizes meritocracy, he rejects Plato's undemocratic ideal:

> [L]acking the perception of the uniqueness of every individual, his incommensurability with others, and consequently not recognizing that a society might change and yet be stable, his doctrine of limited powers and classes came in net effect to the idea of the subordination of individuality. (MW 9, p. 97)

Plato reduces unique incommensurable individuality to a few predetermined social roles thereby sacrificing the individual to society. Dewey further declares that 'in the degree in which society has become democratic, social organization means utilization of the specific and variable qualities of individuals, not stratification by classes' (MW 9, pp. 96–97). Plato offers a planned rather than a planning society.

In contrast to Plato, Rousseau represents the enlightenment era and early modernity in Western history:

> In the eighteenth-century philosophy we find ourselves in a very different circle of ideas. 'Nature' still means something antithetical to existing social organization; Plato exercised a great influence upon Rousseau. But the voice of nature now speaks for the diversity of individual talent and for the need of free development of individuality in all its variety. (MW 9, p. 98)

In this period of transition, Rousseau had an immense impact on debates about the role of education in society. He especially emphasized the need to ground education in 'natural development' and regard 'nature' as the precondition and frame of human life. This was a time of strong tensions between new claims to individualism supported by the emergence of the bourgeois society and the old feudal estate-based society. Rousseau appeals to Nature to criticize the artificial and unjust old order and to point the way toward the democratic reconstructions that would come with the French and other revolutions. Dewey observes the ambivalent character of this appeal to nature and takes pains to appreciate its advantages while criticizing its limitations. He argues that in Rousseau's time, 'the voice of nature … speaks for the diversity of individual talent and for the need of free development of individuality in all its variety. Education in accord with nature furnishes the goal and the method of instruction and discipline' (MW 9, p. 97). It was not possible at that time to conceive of 'individualism' itself as a social construction and of 'individuals' as constructed through interaction and communication in cultural and natural environments. Rather, Rousseau uses nature as conceptual weapon and catchword to defend the claims and rights of individuals against the existing society. Therefore, he 'marred his assertion that education must be a natural development and not something forced or grafted upon individuals from without, by the notion that social conditions are not natural' (MW 9, p. 65). Nevertheless, nature as a theoretical weapon involved a reductionist perspective because all instruments for fighting must be sharp, smooth, and well-polished to be effective. This reduction to effectiveness, however, delimits their scope of possible experiential connections.

Dewey emphasizes an advantage of Froebel's approach is that Froebel recognizes 'the significance of the native capacities of children' (MW 9, p. 63). Dewey appreciates Froebel's 'loving attention to them, and his influence in inducing others to study them' and believes this influence 'represent perhaps the most effective single force in modern educational theory in effecting widespread acknowledgment of the idea of growth' (MW 9, p. 63). But there is also a severe tendency toward reductionism in Froebel's model of education in that he systematically values symbols over experience. 'The result was that Froebel's love of abstract symbolism often got the better of his sympathetic insight; and there was substituted for development as arbitrary and externally imposed a scheme of dictation as the history of instruction has ever seen' (MW 9, p. 64). Dewey's example is the idealization of the symbolic meaning of circles in educational thought and practice:

> A single example may indicate the method. Every one familiar with the kindergarten is acquainted with the circle in which the children gather. It is not enough that the circle is a convenient way of grouping the children. It must be used 'because it is a symbol of the collective life of mankind in general.' (MW 9, p. 63)[1]

It is not that the idea of putting students in a circle is not a good one, but there is no point in consecrating it 'corresponding to the essential traits of the Absolute' (MW 9, p. 62) representing metaphysical ideals like wholeness, harmony, unity, nurturing, initiation, perfection, or completion.

The mixture of religion, myth, and philosophical speculation as contexts of understanding education was especially powerful in the eighteenth and nineteenth centuries in Western societies. Implicitly, it contained equally powerful limits and constraints for meaning-making because Froebel took the symbols literally as given essences or substances and not as meanings constructed from experience. Nevertheless, Froebel's reductionism was not as pervasive with regard to experience of children as was Herbart's who presented a most systematic and rigid form of symbolic reductionism in education. Herbart provided

> a type of theory which denies the existence of faculties and emphasizes the unique role of subject matter in the development of mental and moral disposition: According to it, education is ... the formation of mind by setting up certain associations or connections of content by means of a subject matter presented from without. Education proceeds by instruction taken in a strictly literal sense, a building into the mind from without. (MW 9, p. 75)

Dewey recognizes that with Herbart and his followers teaching was taken seriously as a profession that deserves systematic training, reflection, awareness, and so on, in a time when the school was reconstructed as a social institution and when general schooling was seen as an important advancement in modern society. However, this very approach to general education was connected with strong tendencies to reducing education to the instruction of contents. Dewey observes: 'The fundamental theoretical defect of this view lies in ignoring the existence in a living being of active and specific functions which are developed in the redirection and combination which occur as they are occupied with their environment. The theory represents the Schoolmaster come to his own' (MW 9, p. 77).

Dewey discusses Hegel primarily in a section on 'Education as Unfolding.' While Dewey was a pioneer of developmental educational psychology, it is well known that the aim of education for Dewey is growth, which for him is non-teleological: 'Since growth is the characteristic of life, education is all one with growing; it has no end beyond itself' (MW 9, p. 58). Here is the problem with unfolding:

> Development is conceived not as continuous growing, but as the unfolding of latent powers toward a definite goal. The goal is conceived of as completion, perfection. Life at any stage short of attainment of this goal is merely an unfolding toward it. (MW 9, p. 61)

Dewey is committed to the notion that every individual has unique potential (see Cunningham, 1994). However, he rejects the notion that latent potential merely and by itself unfolds from within. Instead, potentiality is dependent on interactions:

> When the idea that development is due to some indwelling end which tends to control the series of changes passed through is abandoned, potentialities must be thought of in terms of consequences of interactions with other things. Hence potentialities cannot be known till after the interactions have occurred. There are at a given time unactualized potentialities in an individual because and in as far as there are in existence other things with which it has not as yet interacted. (LW 14, p. 109)

By contrast, Hegel starts 'from the conception of a whole—an absolute—which is "immanent" in human life' (MW 9, p. 62). Hegel assumes some perfect *telos* to all development: 'The perfect or complete ideal is not a mere ideal; it is operative here and now. But it is present only implicitly, "potentially," or in an enfolded condition. What is termed development is the gradual making explicit and outward of what is thus wrapped up' (MW 9, p. 62).

For Dewey, ideals can be immensely valuable, but only if they can connect to the actual from whence they were constructed while remaining completely open to criticism and reconstruction. Dewey rejects all *a priori* projects from Plato, to Kant, to Hegel. Instead, we must always start with the customary social practices and embodied habits we have in a given context and then launch projects of critique and reconstruction from there. The problem is that 'in its notion of a complete and all-inclusive end of development, the Hegelian theory swallowed up concrete individualities, though magnifying The Individual in the abstract' (MW 9, p. 65). The main problem with Hegel is that he reduces the concrete unique individual to an abstraction whose only meaning is as a moment in the movement of Spirit to the *Absolute* at the end of history. Insofar as it deviates from this future perfection, it is in error or fallenness. Hence, unique individuality is worse than useless, which is a disaster for Dewey's conception of democracy.

Dewey did not confine his criticisms of reductionism, to historical traditions. He equally addressed developments in his time in theoretical reflection, practical application, and institutional organization. The most important adversary, especially regarding education, was reductionist behaviorism that argued for a narrow focus on causal relations between stimulus and response as observable components of behavior. This approach almost completely forgets emotional, social, and cognitive aspects of experience. Actually, the notorious operant conditioning chamber (also known as the Skinner box) even explicitly excludes such dimensions. Dewey in his criticism of reductionist behaviorism preferred the term conduct over behavior (cf. LW 5, pp. 218–234) because he saw behavior always as part of action in the broader sense of doing and undergoing in experience. He anticipated that reductionist behaviorism would inevitably produce a host of behavior/emotion and behavior/cognition dualisms. More recently, cognitive psychology often tends to do the same with action and emotion. Today, with the constructivist turn that has taken place in recent decades in learning theories world-wide, it seems obvious that such reductionisms cannot do justice to learning processes in their complexity, diversity, and contextually. For many, the term 'New Learning' (cf. Kalantzis & Cope, 2008) and constructivist approaches in learning (cf. Bruner, 1996; Gergen, 2009; Hickman, Neubert, & Reich, 2009) provide contextual perspectives on multi-modal aspects in learning that at least include social, cultural, political, economic dimensions of experience. The affinities to Dewey are apparent. Consider the following:

> Some forms of behaviorism, in reaction against the unnatural isolation of the physical and mental, merely throw the latter overboard entirely, and reduce them to the terms of the material dealt with in purely physical science. In political science may be noted an oscillation between the adoption of non-natural categories, such as a transcendent 'will,' and the resolution of political phenomena into physical terms of conflict and adjustment of forces. A recent economic writer has asserted that economic science has so neglected the place of technology in industry that a generation has gone forth which, although 'educated' in economic science, is almost wholly ignorant of economic affairs. Technology is evidently a matter that connects directly with the development of physical science; the point, instead of being an incidental one, can be shown to be intimately connected with all the sound objections brought against the abstraction of the 'economic man.' The economic man cannot be set in his place in social phenomena, in his actual relations to legal, political, technological and other cultural institutions, until these are connected with natural phenomena. (LW 3, pp. 45–46)

We take this passage from Dewey's essay, 'The inclusive philosophic idea,' in which he favors 'the Social' as the primary category of philosophical reflection. For him, 'interaction' (later 'transaction') is a generic trait of existence. He observes that 'in interactions alone' potentialities are 'released and actualized' (LW 3, p. 41).

Dewey goes on to observe that 'the more numerous and varied the forms of association into which anything enters, the better basis we have for describing and understanding it, for the more complex is an association the more fully are potentialities released for observation' (LW 3, p. 42). A serious problem with reductionist accounts is that they insist upon describing and understanding events in less complex associations. This is so important that we need to pause to say more. Dewey remarks that philosophers are drawn to 'ultimate and unattached simples, called by various writers essences, data, etc.' (LW 3, p. 43). Dewey considers the question of whether we should begin with 'the simple or complex' the most 'important problem in philosophic method at the present time' (LW 3, p. 42). Dewey argues that 'simples' like data, facts, categories, and so on are merely the product of analysis. The critical distinction here is between existence and the essences we socially construct from existence. We must not confuse the products of intellectual analysis with the actual existential events. For instance, Dewey indicates that 'social phenomena are not of themselves, of course, equivalent to social as a category. The latter is derived from the former by means of an intellectual analysis which determines what is their distinctive character' (LW 3, pp. 46–47). These observations lead him to explicitly declare: 'the social, in spite of whatever may be said regarding the temporal and spatial limitation of its manifestations, furnishes philosophically the inclusive category' (LW 3, p. 45). He repeats this conclusion near the end of the essay: 'I do not say that the social as we know it is the whole, but I do emphatically suggest that it is the widest and richest manifestation of the whole accessible to our observation' (LW 3, p. 53). While Dewey wishes to establish genetic continuity in the emergence of properties, he is not guilty of the so-called genetic fallacy, that is, the fallacy that the properties conditioning the origins of something determine all the properties that can emerge as a consequence of its development.[2] With new existential interactions, novel properties may emerge. Reductionism in all its forms fails to recognize emergent transformation, development, and growth.

However, we would call attention to contemporary versions of the old reductionisms and dualisms; for example, in neuroscience where the mind is reduced to the brain, in neuro-linguistics where language is reduced to innate capacities, in neurobiology where social behavior is explained only by neurobiological processes and so on. Such reductionist tendencies are contrary to the core convictions and the main intentions of Dewey's *Democracy and Education*. Therefore, we should be critical with regard to the widespread tendency to adore and overestimate natural sciences and technologies while at the same time underestimating the social and cultural contexts in which they operate. Such reductionist strategies, it seems to us, are increasingly influential in our own time because of the high specialization in scientific culture, the ambivalent and complex nature of liquid modern societies, and the division of labor and compartmentalization of life experiences in current capitalism. Hence, the challenge remains not only to combine the specialized results from different views, but even more importantly to consider and counteract the overall limits of reductionism in order to save a generous understanding of democracy and education. Even if it sounds utopian to overcome compartmentalization and reductionism altogether, the advantage of connecting today with the Deweyan tradition lies in its capability to critically address the limits of specialization and division.

With Dewey, we are convinced that education requires a comprehensive and generous understanding of human experience, learning, and communication in all of its diverse facets. He has an emergent theory of communication with eminent implications for learning theories and practices. Communication involves information, but we must avoid reducing all communication to information processing as is often supposed in contemporary educational theory and practice. Dewey insists that the ultimate value of any communication and institution (social, cultural, economic, political, education) lies in its broad and diverse contributions to making human life experiences more significant and valuable. This gives us a clue for estimating the relative value of natural sciences and technologies in democratic society beyond narrow reductionisms.

3. Reductionism in Contemporary Educational Debates

Against this background, we think Deweyan education today must consider the inevitable tension between necessary democratic claims to social and cultural diversity and capitalist competition. Reductionists often ignore culture and cultural constraints on student learning such as poverty, neighborhood crime, and a parent's level of education. They may also ignore how culture, including the economic system, spirituality, and social security may enable growth. Reductionist approaches like Skinnerian behaviorism usually think of habits as conditioned (or trained) responses to environmental stimuli. What these accounts neglect is, from a Deweyan perspective, that habits are not merely passive adaptations to an existing environment but, at the same time, active powers by which individuals in transactions with others influence, change, transform, and reconstruct their environments as well as themselves.

Especially harmful, in this context, is the effect of generalized measurement on student–teacher relationships and interactions. As we have argued extensively in another place (Garrison, Neubert, & Reich, 2016), one cannot overemphasize the reductionism contained in the rather cold, distanced, 'objective,' and merely instrumental qualities that are supported by excessive and standardized measurement. One-sided orientations to fixed, final, and predefined standards seriously hamper caring, and responsible relationships in learning communities. At the same time, they restrict and seriously reduce the perspectives on the contextual, social, cultural, emotional, creative, and critical dimensions of learning.

For Dewey, it was clear that democracy and education necessarily imply a critical attitude towards selective, partial, and powerful economic and political interests that delimit the processes of learning in society to adaptation to the market and capitalist profits and advantages. Still today, narrow interests appear in perspectives on learning that focus, for example, on 'human capital' and market adaptation for private employment. To the benefit of democracy, we should be educating for the individual, social, creative, critical, and moral growth of democratic citizens instead of merely training standardized interchangeable parts for the global production function. The ideas of 'human capital' and 'one-size-fits-all'-thinking overlook that construction and criticism (cf. LW 5, pp. 125–143) in learning, generously understood, are more productive in the long run than teaching and learning for the test. This applies especially if we consider the necessities of sustainable learning, democratic participation, and educative growth.

Let us take one example from recent global debates on learning. Generally, in our time, we observe a strong will to measurement in education represented among other approaches by PISA i.e. the influential OECD-program for international student assessment. Let us critically consider PISA as representative of other forms of standardized testing. We do so from a Deweyan perspective on experience, learning, and inquiry. It is sufficient here only to think of the well-known five steps in Dewey's model of inquiry, learning, and problem solving.[3]

(i) The necessary first step is 'perplexity' and an emotional response to the situation by the learner. This first condition is often violated in cases of standardized learning and testing like PISA because the very idea of standardization implies neglecting individual and diverse interests and responses. Therefore, all such measures must take refuge in extrinsic motivation from the very outset of their strategies.

(ii) The second step consists of formulating tentative hypotheses constructed from the experience of learners in cooperation with each other, learning materials, and teachers that they then use to construct the problematic situation. This necessarily involves an intellectual response by the learners themselves. Standardized testing leaves very limited space for experimentation with ideas, tentative and imaginative projections, and collaborative ways of developing creative and intelligent perspectives.

(iii) The third step consists of a careful survey (examination, inspection, exploration, and analysis) with regard to the problem. Learners must have occasions for actively exploring problems and their contexts and to constructively gather facts they consider relevant to find solutions. In standardized measurements, by contrast, the program always predefines the problem with very few degrees of freedom for and variation by individual ways of learning. It is often largely decontextualized and does not actually invite or inspire curiosity and joy of exploration. The premium on reproduction in generalized measurement makes creative and experimental approaches highly improbable.

(iv) The transition from the tentative working hypothesis to an explanatory hypothesis based on the constructive work of the learners done in the previous step is an active intellectual refinement of conceptions, observations, imaginations, etc., that again build on skills of communication and cooperation, creativity and experimentation. Standardized testing as a rule leaves only limited opportunities for constructions and deviations concerning the ways of moving from tentative hypotheses to explanatory ideas. In many cases, the program only allows one way of proceeding. In other more intelligent cases, like PISA in this respect, the program at least concedes and values a limited amount of alternatives.

(v) The course of the five steps comes to a provisional, but never final close as learners attempt to solve the problem by acting out and testing their hypotheses.[4] In generalized measurement, this is usually the moment when the paper is taken out of the learners' hands and handed over to somebody who gives summative grades or rankings.

Reductive programs like PISA appear to the public as stable and secure anchors that seem to complete what Dewey calls 'the quest for certainty' (see LW 4) amidst the flux and flow of otherwise confusing and excessively complex realities. We cannot ignore that this very characteristic imbues such programs and the agents who promote them with an immense amount of prestige and power. The hidden curriculum of PISA or other tests influences the role and responsibility of teachers and learners, thereby forming attitudes, expectations, social perceptions, and ways of communication in the classroom. From a pragmatist and constructivist understanding of democracy and education, these are detrimental effects of reductionism because they delimit social and cultural practices, interactions, communication, and learning, and thus counteract educational growth in a broad sense. However, we should see reductionism in all forms as an instrument for a purpose and never as a comprehensive representation of experience. Therefore, we may say that taking the PISA results in their appropriate status as instruments for evaluation and comparative assessment is not by itself harmful as long as we take account of the limits of context and consequence.

On a more general level of public perception, the problem with PISA is that the public largely takes it as a means for representing or copying the entire reality of facts about education. This reductionist mainstream in education (as in other fields) is highly dangerous for democracy. Predominant perspectives on education are always constructions of observers within culture. There is no detached God's perspective or entirely decontextualized permanent neutral framework on education. There are only contingent and falsifiable cultural and individual interpretations. The behaviorist, neuroscientist, neoliberal, or educational specialist participate and act in the context of a specific discursive order with its selective interests, will to truth, and power games that constitute a discipline (see Foucault, 1981). With regard to the complex contexts, however, they often tend to commit the mereological fallacy of mistaking a part for the whole.[5]

Against the background of precarious funding in education everywhere, almost all global societies seem to combine efficiency with feasibility and provide tracks for successful careers. In the background of these attitudes, we often find a general utilitarian approach to education. Therefore, it is hardly surprising that the current compartmentalization is so strong and omnipresent. If we conceive education with Dewey in the broader sense, then the challenge remains to not only to combine the specialized results from different views, but even more importantly to overcome—as far as we can—forms of reductionism to save a generous understanding of democracy and education. Even if it sounds utopian to overcome compartmentalization and reductionism altogether, it seems to us that on the profound level discussed here, one advantage of connecting our situation today with the Deweyan tradition lies in its capability to critically address the limits of specialization and division and its affirmative effects on social realities as given.

For Dewey, we educate only indirectly through the environment in all its complex aspects and dimensions. He argued that learning is an active and constructive process of meaning making in co-constructions with others. To avoid the reduction of learning to mere utility, he accordingly argued for 'greater diversity of capacities' as a regulative ideal for education in modernity: 'The idea of a fixed and single end lying beyond the diversity of human needs and acts rendered utilitarianism incapable of being an adequate representative of the modern spirit' (MW 12, p. 184). Democracy and education claims that we must make the modern ideal of diversity and participation for all strong against the equally modern tendencies to uniformity, order, and utilitarian conformity. The tension between both sides, we may add, is something that we still can observe in our time of liquid modernity.

As to progress in modern society, it remains a deeply ambivalent and unfinished project as long as there is a deep divide between those who can and those who cannot partake in its benefits. Similarly, modern forms of capitalism jeopardize sufficient and sustainable realization of diversity in their tendencies 'to reduce heterogeneity to homogeneity, diversity to sheer uniformity, quality to quantity' (MW 8, p. 7). Construction and criticism in Dewey's sense imply that different, controversial, and even contradictory opinions and reflections are cultivated in educational processes, and that difference and diversity are appreciated as necessary contributions to a democratic way of life. This is the very idea behind his democratic ideal of 'ordered richness' (LW 4, p. 229).

4. Complexity and Reductionism as Educational Challenges Today

We must never neglect the power of markets in contemporary societies, even if we claim with Dewey that we must not confine education to the logic of markets. Against the background of these tensions, the capitalization and the economic narrowing of educational practices and institutions stands against a generous understanding of education as founded in experience in all its diversity and complexity. It leads to homogenization, standardization, generalized testing, will to measure, compartmentalization through selection, ranking, exclusion, and the suppression of difference and diversity. In this context, we think that Deweyan education today must consider the inevitable tension between necessary democratic claims to social and cultural diversity and capitalist competition.

Among other things, capitalism is a powerful context for interpreting nature and culture. Throughout the history of modern society, debates about the relation of naturalism and culturalism have laid the foundations for educational thinking. Capitalism has a tendency to reduce natural as well as social relations to forms of competition and to justify this tendency in terms of nature. Since the second half of the nineteenth century, an important hegemonic discursive formation has accompanied the development of capitalism in modern societies. Social Darwinism attempted to apply the principle of the 'survival of the fittest' and natural selection to social and political thought.[6] We can interpret this ideology as an outgrowth and cultural articulation of the capitalist order, on the one hand, and as a stimulus to further capitalist competition on local, national, as well as global scales. Contained in this development, we find an ecstasy of reductionisms that constitute the very center of the lasting tension between capitalism and democracy. Such reductionisms appear in theory as well as in practice—that is to say in the interpretations of our social and natural world as in our actions in and interactions with it. Under the regime of exchange values, the interpretation of social and natural relations easily reduce to mere striving for profit and interpreting relations as resources for the production of surplus values. The connected practices then often focus on exploitation of nature and human beings. In this context, 'survival of the fittest' simply suggests that the market is just fair for all. The reductionism contained in this thinking has to be made visible by critical public observation and counter-discourses that point to the losses, dark sides, victims, and losers of the allegedly neutral market order like the unemployed, the poor, the left behind, the excluded, and so on. Especially for education, it is necessary to overcome the simplifying logic of such reductionisms. This is one of the reasons, to our minds, why the Deweyan starting point for educational philosophy, namely experience in its generous social and cultural sense, is so important.

The impact of social Darwinism in the culture of modern society, though, is broader than merely a justification of laissez-faire capitalism. It has also been used to support eugenics and racism up to the holocaust. It is important to note that Dewey was never an adherent of social Darwinism. Despite the use of the label 'Darwinism,' the ideas of social Darwinism are almost entirely due to Herbert Spencer. In his essay, 'The philosophical work of Herbert Spencer,' Dewey insists that we must strive 'not only to understand the independence of Spencer's and Darwin's work in relation to each other, but the significance of this independence' (MW 3, p. 205). Dewey specifically mentions Spencer's false notion that evolution was teleological such that social progress is always assured, Spencer's emphasis on atomistic individualism (Darwinian evolution concerns populations), laissez-faire theory, complete distrust of government, and the reading of Spencer's social and political cultural values back into nature as if they arose there. He might have added that Spencer was a Lamarckian; hence, not a Darwinian at all. Dewey does indicate that 'whatever all this is, it is *not* evolution' (MW 3, p. 209). The turn to social Darwinism consists in the idea that the important thing is not success of the multitude of life but elimination of those who are less fortunate and advantaged. It reduces evolution to a rigid and hierarchical scheme in which the 'strong' and powerful dominate and subjugate and ultimately even eliminate the 'weak.' Accordingly, fitness loses its biological Darwinian sense of adaptation to an environment and becomes a social and cultural affair of ranking that often builds on forms of symbolic or physical violence. Whereas Darwin thought fitness in terms of adaption, specialization, mutation, and reproduction, the social Darwinist appropriation of the term focuses on physical strength, health, robustness, force, assertiveness, and violence.

If we draw a more general conclusion from the critical approach to social Darwinism in the wake of Dewey's philosophy of democracy, we may say that reductive claims to homogeneity are as detrimental to democracy and education as arbitrary deregulation and destruction of social orientations and standards that guarantee democratic living together. Against this background, it seems clear that in Dewey's as well as in our time, the discourse of the survival *of the fittest* is not only reductionist, but deeply incompatible with democracy and education. This applies on the global level and has many historical ramifications like colonialism, classism, racism, patriarchy, nationalism, chauvinism, etc. that have as a common denominator the ordering and ranking of the social world according to a scale of strong and weak (cf. Hall, 1996).

At the same time, we must realize with Dewey that we cannot build democracy and education from scratch without taking the powerful contexts of modernity and capitalism seriously into account. This is why the issue of complexity and reductionism is so fundamentally important for educational philosophy. Dewey's life-long critical attitude toward laissez-faire capitalism should be a reminder for us to question reductionist perspectives on nature like social-Darwinist ideologies. In accord with a pragmatist understanding of the intelligent reconstruction of theories and practices, we must always consider the contexts in which we observe, participate, and act. We cannot just invent those contexts out of our heads; we must pay regard to the experience that these contexts condition and partly delimit our capacities of observation, participation, and action. The very idea of reconstruction presupposes that we can overcome the limits only after we have recognized them as actual problems. While we may not simply overcome the dangers of reductionism to education, we must at least try to respond to it by construction and criticism (cf. LW 5, pp. 125–144). The tensional relation between democracy and capitalism constitutes a major challenge for educational philosophy in our own time as much as in Dewey's.

We have dedicated our argumentation to the task of laying out some important theoretical frames and perspectives for criticizing reductionism in education. Given Dewey's basic concepts of experience, habit, and communication in education, we may say that it is a pervasive trait of modernity that it often compartmentalizes social life and social experience by reducing them to fixed categories. Such compartmentalization and reduction have become habitual and formed in institutional ways. The habits of reductionist compartmentalization influence our research and outlook on education.

With Dewey, we may draw two general conclusions for educational philosophy. These conclusions identify two very influential fallacies that we must address and overcome if we want to critically approach reductionisms.

(1) The first very general philosophical fallacy arises out of ignoring contexts. 'I should venture to assert that the most pervasive fallacy of philosophic thinking goes back to neglect of context' (LW 6, p. 5). Dewey mentions several instances including the 'analytic fallacy' that arises whenever the tendency prevails to dissolve existential reality into distinct and isolated units and to treat these elements not as results constructed within the contexts of inquiry, but as something final and independent (LW 6: 6ff). When we recognize the temporal as well as the spatial aspects of context, we arrive at 'the philosophic fallacy' by which Dewey means the 'conversion of eventual functions into antecedent existence' whether performed on 'behalf of mathematical subsistences,

esthetic essences, the purely physical order of nature, or God' (LW 1, p. 389). According to Dewey, we can never separate the abstract process of thinking from the concrete subject matter that is the constructed product of thought. Dewey is a thoroughgoing constructivist about meaning and knowing. His contextualism allows us to avoid reductionism.

(2) Further, Dewey reminds us to avoid intellectualism. 'By "intellectualism" as an indictment,' he writes, 'is meant the theory that all experiencing is a mode of knowing, and that all subject-matter, all nature, is, in principle, to be reduced and transformed till it is defined in terms identical with the characteristics presented by refined objects of science as such' (LW 1, p. 28). We sustain many relations to existence, including confusion, joy, malaise, despair, tragedy, comedy, fear, hope, and reverence. Knowledge allows us to mediate our complex web of relationships to existence. Dewey appreciates the role of intelligence in human affairs, but he criticizes the reduction of experience exclusively to what is known. The problem for education is that intellectualism leads us to focus excessively on cognitive development while neglecting the importance of emotional, esthetic, social, and even moral development.

From the perspective of Cologne interactive constructivism (see e.g. Garrison, 2008; Garrison, Neubert, & Reich, 2012, Ch. 4; Neubert, 2009; Reich, 2009), the distinction between observer, participant, and agent positions can be helpful in explaining why reductionist positions seem to be seductive as well as effective and at the same time to criticize their dominance. To take the complexity of education and culture seriously, it is important to distinguish between the perspectives of observation, participation, and action, and to consider these three perspectives in their necessary interdependence and mutual effects. This is a basic claim in the program of interactive constructivism and it resonates well with Dewey's overall educational philosophy. In consequence, we may equally argue that any of these three roles alone may lead to a reductionist understanding of education, learning, and culture if we only take one in perspective and forget about the others. A narrow focus only on observation (as it can be found in a great deal of educational research and theory) easily leads to a merely subjectivist understanding of education and learning. A narrow focus only on participation overemphasizes a one-sided adaptive and affirmative understanding of socialization. A narrow focus only on action reduces experience to doing for the sake of doing without taking larger conditions and consequences into account. Teachers and learners who partake in procedures of standardized measurement must cultivate not only an ironical attitude toward the limits and apparent claims of this reductionist practice (as observers), but also struggle for conditions and opportunities of educational growth beyond the mere will to measurement (as agents).

Our interactive constructivist approach is in accord with and even continues Dewey's basic philosophical attitude toward the world in which we live. He urges us to encounter our world experimentally as an open universe that allows for many possible perspectives and interpretations. This philosophical approach rejects narrow reductionisms as well as overgeneralizations or willful universalizations. As Bill Gavin puts it:

The pragmatic theory of democracy recognizes that the only universal is in the particular, as Dewey noted. The rejection of certainty as a form of intolerance and the affirmation of pluralism teaches us humility. This point is often underemphasized in Dewey's work. Certainty breeds totalitarianism. Its opposite is uncertainty, better termed 'contextualism.' (Gavin in Green, Neubert, & Reich, 2012, p. 206)

Acknowledgments

We would like to thank the two anonymous reviewers for their helpful comments in improving this paper.

Disclosure statement

No potential conflict of interest was reported by the author(s).

Notes

1. The part of this passage in quotes is citing Froebel.
2. Darwinism is the most famous application of the genetic method. Dewey drew extensively on it in naturalizing Hegel. Gould and Vrba (1982) first exposited the now widely accept idea of 'exaptation,' which is the process by which structures originally selected or adapted to perform one function evolve to perform entirely different functions. We may extend the same idea to the evolution of cultural structures, meanings, and values.
3. We take following argumentation of a larger theoretical context in our book Garrison et al. (forthcoming).
4. Separating the process of inquiry into separate five phases is solely for the analytic purposes of distinguishing the most prominent aspects of the process. As Dewey himself says, 'No set rules can be laid down on such matters;' moreover, there 'is nothing especially sacred about the number five.'
5. Mereology studies the relations of part to whole and the relations of part to part within a whole.
6. For the history of Social Darwinism in America compare Hofstadter (1944/1992, especially Ch. 2).

JOHN DEWEY'S DEMOCRACY AND EDUCATION IN AN ERA OF GLOBALIZATION

References

Bruner, J. S. (1996). *The culture of education*. Cambridge, MA: Harvard University Press.

Cunningham, C. (1994). Unique potential: A metaphor for John Dewey's later conception of the self. *Educational Theory, 44*, 211–224.

Dewey, J.: Collected works. Edited by J. A. Boydston: The early works (EW 1-5): 1882–1898. Carbondale & Edwardsville: Southern Illinois University Press/London & Amsterdam: Feffer & Simons.

Dewey, J.: Collected works. Edited by J. A. Boydston: The middle works (MW 1-15): 1899–1924. Carbondale & Edwardsville: Southern Illinois University Press/London & Amsterdam: Feffer & Simons.

Dewey, J.: Collected works. Edited by J. A. Boydston: The later works (LW 1-17): 1925–1953. Carbondale & Edwardsville: Southern Illinois University Press/London & Amsterdam: Feffer & Simons.

Foucault, M. (1981). The order of discourse. In R. Young (Ed.), *Untying the text: A post-structural anthology* (pp. 48–78). Boston, MA: Routledge & Kegan Paul.

Garrison, J. (Ed.). (2008). *Reconstructing democracy, recontextualizing Dewey. Pragmatism and interactive constructivism in the twenty-first century*. New York, NY: State of the University of New York Press.

Garrison, J., Neubert, S., & Reich, K. (2012). *John Dewey's philosophy of education*. New York, NY: Palgrave.

Garrison, J., Neubert, S., & Reich, K. (2016). *Democracy and education reconsidered. Dewey after one-hundred years*. New York, NY: Routledge.

Gergen, K. (2009). *An invitation to social construction* (2nd ed.). London: Sage.

Gould, S. J. & Vrba, E. S. (1982). Exaptation – A missing term in the science of form. *Paleobiology, 8*, 4–15.

Green, J. M., Neubert, S., & Reich, K. (Eds.). (2012). *Pragmatism and diversity - Dewey in the context of late twentieth century debates*. New York, NY: Palgrave Macmillan.

Hall, S. (1996). The west and the rest: Discourse and power. In S. Hall, D. Held, D. Hubert, & K. Thompson (Eds.), *Modernity: An introduction to modern societies* (pp. 184–227). Malden, MA: Blackwell.

Hickman, L., Neubert, S., & Reich, K. (Eds.). (2009). *John Dewey between pragmatism and constructivism*. New York, NY: Fordham.

Hofstadter, R. (1944/1992). *Social Darwinism in American thought*. Boston, MA: Beacon Press.

Kalantzis, M., & Cope, B. (2008). *New learning*. Cambridge: Cambridge University Press.

Neubert, S. (2009). Pragmatism, constructivism, and the theory of culture. In L. Hickman, S. Neubert, & K. Reich (Eds.), *John Dewey between pragmatism and constructivism* (pp. 162–184). New York, NY: Fordham.

Reich, K. (2009). Observers, participants, and agents in discourses. In L. Hickman, S. Neubert, & K. Reich (Eds.), *John Dewey between pragmatism and constructivism* (pp. 106–142). New York, NY: Fordham.

Not 'democratic education' but 'democracy and education': Reconsidering Dewey's oft misunderstood introduction to the philosophy of education

JOHN QUAY

Abstract

Of enduring interest to philosophers of education is the intimate connection Dewey draws between Democracy and Education *in this now century-old seminal work. At first glance the connection may appear quite simple, with the two terms commonly combined today as 'democratic education'. But there is significantly more to Dewey's connection between democracy and education than 'democratic education' suggests. Evidence for this greater depth can be seen in Dewey's choice of subtitle for his text:* an introduction to the philosophy of education. *In this article I illuminate some of the further riches Dewey offered to understanding democracy and education, central to which is his theorization of 'occupations' as this aligns with his attempts to articulate a 'coherent theory of experience'. As with democracy and education, the educational import of occupations cannot be captured with a mere combination of terms as in 'vocational education'. In both cases we are simply appending an adjective to education, which Dewey found problematic. What we need, he argued, is a sense of education 'pure and simple' with 'no qualifying adjectives prefixed'. An existential consideration of occupations enables just that, wherein occupations define the functional unities of life, the character of social groupings, the ways in which growth is arranged. As such they provide us with new ways of conceptualizing the structure of schools and the nature of learning. Here, democracy and education come together in a much more fundamental sense as expressions of life.*

The Experiential Heart of *Democracy and Education*

Dewey's *Democracy and Education* did not suddenly appear as if from no-where at no-time. The book was a significant achievement in its own right, but it was also part of an ongoing project through which Dewey aimed to offer a philosophy which would draw together four developments he saw as central to the future of American society. In the preface to *Democracy and Education* he proclaimed that 'the philosophy stated in this book connects the growth of democracy with the development of the experimental method in the sciences, evolutionary ideas in the biological sciences, and the industrial reorganization' (1916/1972, p. 4).[1] These four—democracy, scientific method, evolutionary ideas, industrial reorganization—were the developments which Dewey believed contributed most significantly to the ebbs and flows which marked American society. While most Americans did their best just to stay afloat in this turbulent current, Dewey sought to understand it, and through such understanding to harness it such that society could be improved—through education.

In this article I focus on what Dewey hoped to achieve through the publication of *Democracy and Education* and why—by highlighting the nature of the relation between democracy and education that he was promulgating. While today we commonly express the connection between democracy and education via various forms of democratic education, I argue that this clouds what Dewey had in mind, as democratic education can be construed as the offering of just another form of education among others, such as sustainability education, physical education, civics and citizenship education. My searching reveals only one instance where Dewey writes specifically about democratic education, perhaps signaling that this was not what he was chiefly about. This reference appears in an essay concerning the student revolt in China in May 1919, wherein Dewey mentions 'a democratic education' (1920/1972, p. 25) as a form of strategy, endorsed through this student movement, as a means to best secure China's sovereignty.

Instead of just adding democratic education to the growing list of various forms of education, I suggest that with *Democracy and Education* Dewey was attempting to indicate a broad direction which education, all education, should follow, if paying heed to the current of change—democracy, scientific method, evolutionary ideas, industrial reorganization—which was reforming American society. Education itself should be similarly reformed, reconstructed, reorganized, such that it could be part of, and contribute positively to, the ongoing changes being experienced.

Dewey's project did not, of course, conclude with *Democracy and Education*. By referencing another of Dewey's seminal texts in education, one which he published more than twenty years later—*Experience and Education*—we can gain a better sense of the importance of experience to the broad direction of reform Dewey was indicating for education in *Democracy and Education*. In the second half of this article I bring both texts together, along with much of Dewey's other philosophical work, to illuminate 'a sound philosophy of experience' (1938a/1985, p. 63) or 'coherent theory of experience' (p. 16) in comprehending the direction for educational reform he was attempting to convey. This direction, with experience at its core, was stated in *Democracy and Education*.

> The advance of psychology, of industrial methods, and of the experimental method in science makes another conception of experience explicitly desirable and possible. This theory reinstates the idea of the ancients that

experience is primarily practical, not cognitive—a matter of doing and undergoing the consequences of doing. But the ancient theory is transformed by realizing that doing may be directed so as to take up into its own content all which thought suggests, and so as to result in securely tested knowledge. 'Experience' then ceases to be empirical and becomes experimental. Reason ceases to be a remote and ideal faculty, and signifies all the resources by which activity is made fruitful in meaning. Educationally, this change denotes such a plan for the studies and method of instruction as has been developed in the previous chapters. (Dewey, 1916/1972, p. 286)

A sound philosophy of experience sits at the heart of Dewey's project because experience affords intimate connection between theory (reason) and practice. A significant challenge Dewey faced with his philosophical work was that of maintaining association between theory and practice—of distilling theoretical understanding from practice which could then be applied in future practice—a struggle that characterized his own life. 'I imagine my development has been controlled largely by a struggle between a native inclination toward the schematic and formally logical, and those incidents of personal experience that compelled me to take account of actual material' (1930a/1985, p. 151). The four developments—democracy, scientific method, evolutionary ideas, industrial reorganization—were key features of Dewey's personal experience, compelling him to take account of them philosophically, theoretically, in a way which he hoped would inform practice, especially educational practice.

It is worth noting that Dewey's personal experience was characterized by a maelstrom of change. Democracy, scientific method, evolutionary ideas, and industrial reorganization were all implicated in the significant differences that distinguished American society in the year of Dewey's birth (1859) from that marked by the publication of *Democracy and Education* (1916) more than fifty years later. 'The things once made at home were now made in factories and the child knew nothing of them. The inventions and discoveries in science brought railroads, the telegraph and telephone, gas and electricity, farm machinery' (Dewey, 1933a/1985, p. 150). These developments supported an 'industrialization' which 'brought the big city' into being, along 'with its slums and palaces, its lack of play space, its sharp distinction between city and country' (p. 150). Such industrialization impacted family life, especially via increasing access to the

> automobile, the movies and the radio, with their enormous influence in taking the family out of the home and making even the little child much more part of the great world than had ever been dreamed of in the past. (p. 150)

Dewey (1927/1985) argued that such 'technological discoveries and inventions' worked 'a change in the customs by which men [sic] had been bound together'; thus they were entangled with 'the transition from family and dynastic government supported by the loyalties of tradition[,] to popular government' (p. 327). He was clear that this transition toward democracy 'was not due to the doctrines of doctrinaires' (p. 327); it was not a progression brought about by those peddling ideas of democracy—it was much more complex than that. The familiar features of 'democratic governments,' he noted, 'represent the cumulative effect of a multitude of events, unpremeditated as far as political effects were concerned and having unpredictable consequences' (p. 327). This is an important point because it suggests that there 'is no [inherent] sanctity in universal suffrage, frequent elections, majority rule, congressional and cabinet government' (p. 327), the main features of American democratic government. Instead, these developments were aspects of the broader 'direction in which the current was moving' and so involved only 'a minimum of departure from antecedent custom and law' (p. 327). Their purpose was 'that of meeting existing needs which had become too intense to ignore,' rather 'than that of forwarding the democratic idea' (p. 327) per se.

Dewey's own experience told him that democracy as a form of community life was growing, changing, and education should grow with it. This is 'the challenge that democracy offers to education', a challenge born in the understanding that 'democracy in order to live must change and move' (1937/1985, p. 183). Hence 'the greatest mistake that we can make about democracy is to conceive of it as something fixed, fixed in idea and fixed in its outward manifestation' (p. 183). The same, of course, applied to education, as both were co-implicated. 'Democracy cannot endure, much less develop, without education in that narrower sense in which we ordinarily think of it, the education that is given in the family, and especially as we think of it in the school' (1938b/1985, p. 297).

Dewey sought to engage pragmatically, in the way he employed this term, with this experience of change wrought by developments in democracy, scientific method, evolutionary ideas, and industrial reorganization. His pragmatic approach involved positioning practical issues philosophically, on the basis that 'philosophic problems arise because of widespread and widely felt difficulties in social practice' (1916/1972, p. 383). *Democracy and Education* is a philosophical work; and Dewey later described it as the book which 'was for many years that in which my philosophy, such as it is, was most fully expounded' (1930a/1985, p. 157). However, this philosophical work was also Dewey's articulation of a theory of education, highlighted by the rarely quoted subtitle he chose: *an introduction to the philosophy of education*. He considered 'the educational point of view' to enable 'one to envisage the philosophic problems where they arise and thrive, where they are at home, and where acceptance or rejection makes a difference in practice' (1916/1972, p. 383). It was in education that he saw the developments in democracy, scientific method, evolutionary ideas and industrial reorganization coming to expression both theoretically and practically. With this in mind he proclaimed that 'philosophy is the theory of education as a deliberately conducted practice' (p. 387).

However, while in *Democracy and Education* Dewey was 'concerned to point out the changes in subject matter and method of education *indicated* by these developments' (1916/1972, p. 4, italics added), it was not his intention to offer a detailed program of educational practice in the book. This was not a concrete recipe for a democratic education. Rather it was a philosophic understanding education could and should embrace if the changes being experienced in American society were heeded philosophically. It was a theory of education, an introduction to the philosophy of education. Specific changes in educational practice involving subject matter and method would then, he hoped, flow from this new understanding. And they did so in specific and well-publicized cases (see Dewey & Dewey, 1915/1972). But these practical initiatives were in no way broad-based, for the changes in educational theory he proposed came up against a more general form of educational practice founded in a very different understanding.

When New Theory Encounters Old Practice

Dewey's philosophical emphasis in *Democracy and Education* was the source of some confusion in relation to interpretations of this work. Few philosophers read it and most educators didn't understand it. He noted fifteen years or so after its publication that he was unsure whether 'philosophic critics, as distinct from teachers, have ever had recourse to it' (1930a/1985, p. 157). This lack of impact in the philosophical world may be partially attributed to its publication in a 'textbook series' (Young, 1916, p. 6) in education. In her review of the book for *The Journal of Education* Young provided an educator's perspective, noting that 'it is radically different from the jejune writing sometimes set before teachers as education' (p. 6). Another review written for *The Elementary School Journal* advised that 'one should distinguish, as he [*sic*] reads Professor Dewey's book, between a general philosophy of education and a practical application of this philosophy in school organization'; because 'this distinction is not made by Professor Dewey, and undoubtedly would not be regarded by him as necessary' (1916, p. 14). Dewey's subtitle had signaled this distinction, but few teachers comprehended it.

Assuming the merit of Dewey's ideas, a major issue standing in the way of their practical translation was the contrast between the consequences he envisaged (but didn't clearly articulate) and the traditional version of schooling he often critiqued. Kliebard (2006) notes that 'many of the educational ideas that Dewey set forth in *Democracy and Education* and elsewhere were profoundly incompatible with existing structures of schooling' (p. 126). Translation of Dewey's ideas demanded a shift in practice that many teachers struggled to envisage. In her review of the book, Young (1916) commented that its appeal 'to experience hither-to undescribed' may lead some to the judgement 'that it is impossible for class purposes' (p. 6). Many teachers naturally struggled to imagine teaching and school organization in ways other than those they were familiar with; likewise parents, who may be even more conservative than teachers when it comes to school reform.

As Biesta (2010) shrewdly recognizes, 'this begins to explain why there is relatively little in Dewey's work that tells us how we should educate for democracy' (p. 214). Dewey was concerned with articulating a theoretical position that *indicated* changes in educational practice accruing from the connections he drew between education and the growth of democracy, the development of the experimental method in the sciences, evolutionary ideas in the biological sciences, and the industrial reorganization—but he did not attempt to fully describe or prescribe these changes. This 'also explains why Dewey does not really have a theory of democratic education' (p. 214), if by this we mean a theory of the practice of a form of education deemed democratic.

A corresponding issue Dewey faced was the coherence (or lack of) of his own theory, a coherence he deemed necessary for achievement of his educational project, a coherence which was the very definition of philosophy as 'a theory of truth, reality, or experience, taken as an organized whole, and so giving rise to general principles which unite the various branches or parts of experience into a coherent unity' (1902a/1972, p. 192). This coherent unity was not to be found specifically in theories of democracy or education but rather in a theory of experience, which he considered more basic. Thus any 'practical attempts to develop schools based upon the idea that education is found in life-experience are bound to exhibit inconsistencies and confusions unless they are guided by some conception of what experience is' (1938a/1985, p. 32). As such, 'a coherent *theory* of experience, affording positive direction to selection and organization of appropriate educational methods and materials, is required by the attempt to give new direction to the work of the schools' (p. 16, italics in original).[2]

Piecing Together a Coherent Theory of Experience

If Dewey's philosophy of education was to have the significant consequences for schooling which he hoped, then it needed to hang together in such a way as to enable teachers and administrators to translate it into a coherent set of practices. Theory and practice would then consistently support each other in a new version of the 'reciprocal relation' between 'democracy and education' (1938c/1985, p. 297), undercutting the many criticisms aimed at educational reforms. Dewey recognized that such an educational theory needed to be basic, to get down to the fundamentals of education, what he (1938a/1985) called 'the nature of education with no qualifying adjectives prefixed' (p. 63). He was not interested in identifying another version or form of education, one among other forms. Instead, 'what we want and need is education pure and simple, and we shall make surer and faster progress when we devote ourselves to finding out just what education is' (p. 63). 'It is for this reason alone,' he stressed, 'that I have emphasized the need for a sound philosophy of experience' (p. 63). For Dewey, 'finding out just what education is' was dependent on 'a sound philosophy of experience.' He made the call for such a theory in his last book length treatise on education, *Experience and Education*, but he was aware of the issues with experience and the consequences for education much earlier, back at the turn of the century, well before publication of *Democracy and Education*.

> Having no sense of the unity of experience, and of the definitive relation of each branch of study to that unity, we have no criterion by which to judge and decide. We yield to popular pressure and clamor; first on the side of the instinct for progress, and then on the side of the habit of inertia. As a result, every movement, whether for nature study or spelling, for picture study or arithmetic, for manual training or more legible handwriting, is treated as an isolated and independent thing. It is this separation, this vital lack of unity, which leads to the confusion and contention which are so marked features of the educational situation. Lacking a philosophy of unity, we have no basis upon which to make connections, and our whole treatment

becomes piecemeal, empirical and at the mercy of external circumstances. (Dewey, 1902b/1972, p. 266)

So how to approach this task of developing a coherent theory of experience? It is my contention that through his rich commentary on experience, spanning many decades of philosophical thought, Dewey had articulated the makings of a sound philosophy of experience, often repeating aspects in writings published many years apart, which illuminate the ongoing nature of his project. However, he did not succeed in bringing the various pieces of the jigsaw together in one place so as to share a fuller picture. This is a task I shall attempt in the remainder of this article, with the aim being to offer a consideration of Dewey's educational theory such that the reciprocal relation between democracy and education is advanced somewhat, at least on the educational side (see also Quay, 2013, 2015; Quay & Seaman, 2013).

In *Democracy and Education* Dewey penned a chapter on 'experience and thinking', the first section of which he titled 'the nature of experience' (1916/1972, p. 147). The main point conveyed in this section is that experience is transactional. 'We do something to the thing and then it does something to us in return' (p. 147). In another account of this same point made much later, Dewey suggested that 'an experience is always what it is because of a transaction taking place between an individual and what, at the time, constitutes his [sic] environment' (1938a/1985, p. 26). The environment here can have many manifestations, all of which pertain to the transaction, for example the environment may consist of

> persons with whom he [the individual] is talking[,] about some topic or event, the subject talked about being also part of the situation; or the toys with which he is playing; the book he is reading (in which his environing conditions at the time may be England or ancient Greece or an imaginary region); or the materials of an experiment he is performing. (p. 26)

This transactional view of experience has ramifications for 'the educator for whom the problems of democracy are at all real', highlighting the necessity for 'making the connection between the child and his [sic] environment as complete and intelligent as possible, both for the welfare of the child and for the sake of the community' (1915/1972, p. 390).

Understanding the nature of experience as transactional is a beginning which Dewey built on in the next section in this same chapter on experience and thinking, titled 'reflection in experience': for 'thought or reflection ... is the discernment of the relation between what we try to do and what happens in consequence' (1916/1972, p. 152). In other words, thought enables us to attribute meaning to these transactions. Dewey labeled this 'reflective experience' and listed its 'general features' (p. 158).

> They are (*i*) perplexity, confusion, doubt, due to the fact that one is implicated in an incomplete situation whose full character is not yet determined; (*ii*) a conjectural anticipation—a tentative interpretation of the given elements, attributing to them a tendency to effect certain consequences; (*iii*) a careful survey (examination, inspection, exploration, analysis) of all

attainable consideration which will define and clarify the problem in hand; (iv) a consequent elaboration of the tentative hypothesis to make it more precise and more consistent, because squaring with a wider range of facts; (v) taking one stand upon the projected hypothesis as a plan of action which is applied to the existing state of affairs: doing something overtly to bring about the anticipated result, and thereby testing the hypothesis. (Dewey, 1916/1972, p. 158)

This was not the first time Dewey had articulated these features. They first appeared (as far as I can tell) in a chapter of a book he edited titled *Studies in Logical Theory* (1903/1972, p. 308); reappearing in the first edition of *How We Think* (1910/1972, pp. 237–238); then in *Democracy and Education*; then in the revised edition of *How We Think* (1933b/1985, pp. 200–210); and finally in *Logic: The Theory of Inquiry* (1938b/1985, pp. 110–121). Each iteration contains the same steps or phases, sometimes five and other times condensed as four.

While he presented these features as steps or phases Dewey was adamant that 'the sequence of the five phases is not fixed' (1933b/1985, p. 207); they are not merely a mechanical routine. A further internal pattern to these steps illuminates the more complex relations between them. Dewey identified 'two types of [reflective] experience according to the proportion of reflection found in them' (1916/1972, p. 152). One of these involved steps three and four, 'for it is the extent and accuracy of steps three and four which mark off a distinctive reflective experience from one on the trial and error plane' (p. 158). The other less reflective type of reflective experience is thus basic trial and error. 'We simply do something, and when it fails, we do something else, and keep on trying till we hit upon something which works, and then we adopt that method as a rule of thumb measure in subsequent procedure' (pp. 152–153). This still involves thinking (as reflection) but in a minimalist way, not accessing the distinctive reflective experience of steps three and four, which are bypassed in favor of action supported by reduced reflection. As such, this trial and error type of reflective experience is embraced within steps two and five (see Figure 1).

This suggests that engaging in a distinctive reflective experience—which is an abstract or theoretical type reflection in contrast to the more practical and concrete reflection of steps two and five (see Dewey, 1933b/1985, pp. 300–301)—is optional. In addition, any engagement in abstract reflection must return through the concrete step five in order to trial the ideas developed through steps three and four. Thus 'we never get wholly beyond the trial and error situation' as 'our most elaborate and rationally consistent thought has to be tried in the world and thereby tried out' (1916/1972, pp. 158–159).

This leaves just step one to account for; a seemingly insignificant step that is actually of great importance because it highlights a mode of experience which is not reflective. This step describes the 'starting point of any process of [reflective] thinking' where there 'is something going on, something which just as it stands is incomplete or unfulfilled' (1916/1972, p. 154). This incompleteness is 'a felt difficulty' (1910/1972, p. 237). It is 'the dawning of the problem', any problem, before which 'no problem

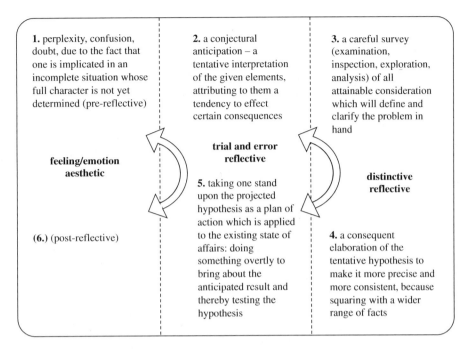

Figure 1: Dewey's general features of reflective experience showing the pattern that exists revealing the place of aesthetic experience and the two types of reflective experience.

or difficulty in the quality of the experience has presented itself to provoke reflection' (1903/1972, p. 308). This dawning does not, therefore, occur in reflective experience. Dewey (1929/1985) argued that reflective or 'cognitive experience must originate within that of a non-cognitive [non-reflective] sort' (p. 31). And not only must it originate here, but it must also end in this non-cognitive form of experience. Hence, Dewey (1933b/1985) described 'two limits of every unit of [reflective] thinking': 'a perplexed, troubled, or confused situation at the beginning and a cleared-up, unified, resolved situation at the close' (p. 200). The first he designated '*pre*-reflective' and the second '*post*-reflective' (p. 201). It is this post-reflective situation that I label as step six.

A key characteristic of this non-reflective experience is that it concerns the quality of the experience, which means the feel of the experience. It is that mode of experience wherein there is no issue significant enough to warrant engaging reflection, be that trial and error or distinctive reflective experience. But this doesn't mean that in these moments when things are going along smoothly, when we are not reflecting, that we are not thinking. In these moments there is still a felt awareness of what is going on, of the qualitative character of the situation. Dewey referred to this as 'affective thought' (1926/1985, p. 105) or 'qualitative thought' (1930b/1985, p. 251). Important here is the quality, the feeling, the emotion, some form of which is always with us. It is in this sense that Dewey called this non-reflective experience 'esthetic experience' (1950/1985, p. 396).[3]

> Esthetic experience is experience in its integrity. Had not the term 'pure' been so often abused in philosophic literature, had it not been so often employed to suggest that there is something alloyed, impure, in the very nature of experience and to denote something beyond experience, we might say that esthetic experience is pure experience. For it is experience freed from the forces that impede and confuse its development as experience; freed, that is, from factors that subordinate an experience as it is directly had to something beyond itself. To esthetic experience, then, the philosopher must go to understand what experience is. (Dewey, 1934/1985, p. 279)

Aesthetic experience is not about pleasure, beauty, or taste in the way we tend to use this term today. Rather it plays on the notion of perception, which is the Greek root of the word. Our basic perceptive awareness is feeling orientated, it is emotional. Dewey (1934/1985, p. 50) argued that 'emotion is the moving and cementing force' in experience. 'It selects what is congruous and dyes what is selected with its color, thereby giving qualitative unity to materials externally disparate and dissimilar. It thus provides unity in and through the varied parts of an experience' (p. 50). And 'when the unity is of the sort already described [qualitative unity], the experience has esthetic character' (p. 50).

We thus have two basic modes of experience: aesthetic experience and reflective experience. But Dewey was also clear that 'esthetic [experience] cannot be sharply marked off from intellectual experience since the latter must bear an esthetic stamp to be itself complete' (1934/1985, p. 46). In other words, when we engage with reflective experience because trying to resolve some problem or issue, the qualitative character of the situation continues to flavor the reflective experience. In addition, we can't sharply mark off distinctive reflective experience from that of the trial and error type because the practical contingencies continue to assert themselves. We engage with reflective experience in order to resolve some issue that emerged within aesthetic experience, and this issue is always of a practical nature—even if it might appear to be purely academic or theoretical. After all, academic issues are alive in the practical world of academics. This suggests a nested relationship between these modes and types of experience (see Figure 2).

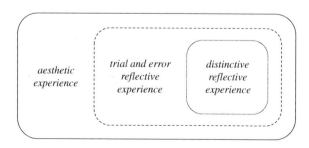

Figure 2: The nested relationship between aesthetic experience and the two types of reflective experience.

A Coherent Theory of Experience and its Connection with Practice through Occupations

Dewey never clearly articulated a coherent theory of experience in the one place by drawing aesthetic experience and reflective experience together in this way, although it could be argued that he had, all along, stated this coherence through his many expressions of the general features of reflective experience, with its emergence from and return to a non-reflective mode of experience. However, now that we have a Deweyan version of a coherent theory of experience, the challenge becomes one of bringing this theory closer to practice in a form that teachers and administrators can more readily comprehend. To do this I turn to Dewey's notion of occupations, which can be mapped against the nested relationship between aesthetic and reflective experience. I am supported in this move by Dewey's claim that 'education *through* occupations … combines within itself more of the factors conducive to learning than any other method' (1916/1972, p. 320).

In any discussion of Dewey's conception of occupations it is important to clarify the breadth that this notion held for him. Occupations (vocations or callings) were *not* merely adult jobs for Dewey, although these are included in his definition. 'A vocation means nothing but such a direction of life activities as renders them perceptibly significant to a person, because of the consequences they accomplish, and also useful to his associates' (1916/1972, p. 317). Therefore 'we must avoid not only limitation of conception of vocation to the occupations where immediately tangible commodities are produced, but also the notion that vocations are distributed in an exclusive way, one and only one to each person' (p. 318). As an example he presented the case of an artist.

> No one is just an artist and nothing else, and in so far as one approximates that condition, he is so much the less developed human being; he is a kind of monstrosity. He must, at some period of his life, be a member of a family; he must have friends and companions; he must either support himself or be supported by others, and thus he has a business career. He is a member of some organized political unit, and so on. We naturally *name* his vocation from that one of the callings which distinguishes him, rather than from those which he has in common with all others. But we should not allow ourselves to be so subject to words as to ignore and virtually deny his other callings when it comes to a consideration of the vocational phases of education. (Dewey, 1916/1972, p. 318)

The breadth of Dewey's definition suggests that we are always engaged in some occupation, and that there are occupations within occupations: the relation between occupations is a complex one (a point I shall return to in making connections with democracy). In addition to this breadth of application, Dewey also spoke of three basic characteristics of occupations—characteristics which map well against our coherent theory of experience. So if this coherent theory of experience is in any way valid, then occupations must be able to be expressed via aesthetic and reflective experience. In drawing these connections I acknowledge that Dewey did not, to my knowledge, ever clearly do so.

In aligning occupations with aesthetic experience, I proffer Dewey's (1916/1972) argument that 'occupations should be concerned primarily with *wholes*', where 'wholes for purposes of education are not ... physical affairs' (p. 207) as in the ordered presentation of sets of objects or skills to be learned. 'Intellectually the existence of a whole depends upon a concern or interest; it is qualitative, the completeness of appeal made by a situation' (p. 207). Here an occupation, for example being an artist, is lived holistically as an interest which qualitatively characterizes a situation in a particular way. There is, however, much aesthetic nuance and subtlety to this existential occupation. Naming it tends to reify it within reflective experience through application of a very blunt label that seeks to capture and convey (often unsuccessfully) what is a way of living in the moment. There are countless emotional hues that qualify 'being an artist' in aesthetic experience.

In aligning occupations with the trial and error type of reflective experience, I tender Dewey's contention that 'an occupation is a continuous activity having a purpose' (1916/1972, p. 320). Here an occupation is concerned, as trial and error type reflective experience is, with doing, with activity. Trial and error type reflective experience remains within the practice of an occupation. We are reflectively aware of the activity, for example painting, while dealing with issues, large and small, as we continue with the activity in order to achieve its purpose(s).

In aligning occupations with distinctive reflective experience, I put forward Dewey's assertion that 'a calling is also of necessity an organizing principle for information and ideas; for knowledge and intellectual growth' (1916/1972, p. 320). Here an occupation 'provides an axis which runs through an immense diversity of detail; it causes different experiences, facts, items of information to fall into order with one another' (p. 320). Any distinctive reflective experience occurs within an occupation. But a major strength of distinctive reflective experience is that it can move abstractly among different existential occupations, between different ways of knowing and doing that have in some way been experienced, thereby offering the potential to bring other ideas and methods to bear on the issue at hand.

While occupations can be considered quite simplistically as adult jobs, my rendering of Dewey's conception of occupations in connection with his contributions to a coherent theory of experience highlights their complexity. But this daunting existential complexity is made accessible through an understanding of occupations as that 'unity of experience' which Dewey (1902b/1972, p. 266) saw lacking. Occupations encapsulate every aspect of a coherent theory of experience and they thus facilitate a translation of this theory into various forms of practice.

Occupations as the Living Expression of *Democracy and Education*

Occupations are a central feature of Dewey's understanding of experience, of life; so much so that 'occupations ... are essentially social life' (1915/1972, p. 315), for 'occupations bring people naturally together in groups' (1909a/1972, p. 192). These two contentions enable a practical consideration of occupations in connection with Dewey's democratic conception of education, building on his idea that 'a democracy is more than a form of government; it is primarily a mode of associated living, of conjoint communicated experience' (1916/1972, p. 94). Thus a major concern of Dewey's *Democracy and Education* is articulation of 'the two points ... by which to measure the worth of a form of social life': (1) 'the extent in which the interests of a group are shared by all its members', and (2) 'the fullness and freedom with which it interacts with other groups' (1916/1972, p. 106). When we read these two points with occupations in mind, we can see how Dewey's work offers not only a translation of theory into practical application via occupations as the unity of experience, but also a way to judge between occupations, which is crucial for any educational interpretation. This feeds into schooling when we understand that 'the problem and the opportunity with the young is selection of orderly and continuous modes of occupation', occupations which, 'while they lead up to and prepare for the indispensable activities of adult life, have their own sufficient justification in their present reflex influence upon the formation of habits of thought' (Dewey, 1933b/1985, p. 151). This does not mean that we are merely selecting the best adult occupations to teach to young people. No. What we must do as educators is to create occupations which engage the concerns and interests (rich and variable across different ages, cultures, genders, etc.) of children and young people, that harness activity through productive purposes, and which bring knowledge to bear in the resolution of problems encountered. In this way we grow *through* occupations, via the existential urge to *be* that sits at the heart of occupations.

Occupations can be placed at the heart of schooling by employing them as units of study and thereby repositioning the traditional emphasis on knowledge disciplines which gives rise to the main school-based occupation: being an academic student. In this repositioning, occupations come to influence each element of 'the trinity of school': '(1) the life of the school as a social institution in itself; (2) methods of learning and of doing work; and (3) the school studies or curriculum' (Dewey, 1909b/1972, p. 286). They impact on subject matter because they provide an organizing principle for knowledge. They support method because each occupation is a continuous activity having purpose(s). And they can lead to a reorganization of the life of the school as a social institution because they function as the basic unit around which the school is organized—units of study that are connected directly, rather than vicariously, to the lives of children and young people. The complexity associated with this reorganization—offering a myriad of occupations of concern to children and young people—involves continual rethinking because education, as Dewey noted with democracy, is never something fixed. The reciprocal relation between democracy and education then points to further developments in democracy aligned with developments in education. Democracy, as Dewey conceived it, facilitates growth for all people (not just adults) by enabling educative occupations, as forms of social life. As we come to share a better understanding of the unity in experience and education provided by Dewey's conception of occupations, this should engender some change in how we understand and practice democracy, as well as education.

Detailing the finer practical considerations which would need to take place in order to bring this Deweyan dream to reality (beyond some well-designed electives and co-curricular activities) is outside the scope of this article. However, one question remains. Why is it that Dewey did not see these connections and articulate the coherence in his theory which would have greatly assisted its translation into practice? My response to this question is encompassed in two points. The first is that, while he acknowledged that the transition toward democracy 'was not due to the doctrines of doctrinaires' (1927/1985, p. 327), Dewey was at heart a doctrinaire, generally relying on others to trial and experiment with practical applications of his philosophy. The second is that his articulation of occupations was overrun at the time by the easier to comprehend push for vocational education (see Labaree, 2010). Occupations weren't generally perceived as the broad experiential unities of life but rather as adult jobs, with vocational education designed to train young people for them. This battle was going on at the time of publication of *Democracy and Education*, highlighting the importance of this text in promoting a vision for education and for democracy that would take America into the next stage of its evolution as a nation. I would argue that this stage still awaits. But if we can manage to implement some of the practical changes in education that emanate from Dewey's work then it may be around the corner (or perhaps a few corners).

Disclosure statement

No potential conflict of interest was reported by the author.

Notes

1. All page references ascribed to Dewey are to volumes in *The Collected Works of John Dewey, 1882-1853*, as detailed in the reference list. I have included original publication dates with citations of Dewey's writing because the chronological relationship between texts is important to the arguments made in this article.
2. Such talk of coherence may unsettle those who dispute the possibility of philosophical systems. At one point in his career Dewey admitted that while he did not have 'the aversion to system as such' that was sometimes attributed to him, he was 'dubious' of his 'ability to reach inclusive systematic unity' (1930a/1985, p. 156). A decade later he had shifted his position, feeling the need 'to retract disparaging remarks ... made in the past about the need for system in philosophy' because he found 'that with respect to the hanging together of various problems and various hypotheses in a perspective determined by a definite point of view' he did indeed 'have a system' (1940/1985, p. 143).
3. Dewey used two forms of spelling through his work: aesthetic and esthetic. For consistency I shall use aesthetic.

References

Biesta, G. (2010). The most influential theory of the century: Dewey, democratic education, and the limits of pragmatism. In D. Trohler, T. Schlag, & F. Osterwalder (Eds.), *Pragmatism and modernities* (pp. 207–224). Rotterdam: Sense Publishers.

Dewey, J. (1902a/1972). Contributions to Dictionary of Philosophy and Psychology. In J. A. Boydston (Ed.), *The Middle Works of John Dewey, 1899–1924*. (Vol. 2, pp. 140–271). Carbondale: Southern Illinois University Press.

Dewey, J. (1902b/1972). The educational situation. In J. A. Boydston (Ed.), *The Middle Works of John Dewey, 1899–1924* (Vol. 1, pp. 220–314). Carbondale: Southern Illinois University Press.

Dewey, J. (1903/1972). Studies in logical theory. In J. A. Boydston (Ed.), *The Middle Works of John Dewey, 1899–1924* (Vol. 2, pp. 294–383). Carbondale: Southern Illinois University Press.

Dewey, J. (1909a/1972). The bearings of pragmatism on education. In J. A. Boydston (Ed.), *The Middle Works of John Dewey, 1899–1924* (Vol. 4, pp. 189–192). Carbondale: Southern Illinois University Press.

Dewey, J. (1909b/1972). The moral principles in education. In J. A. Boydston (Ed.), *The Middle Works of John Dewey, 1899–1924* (Vol. 4, pp. 266–293). Carbondale: Southern Illinois University Press.

Dewey, J. (1910/1972). How we think. In J. A. Boydston (Ed.), *The Middle Works of John Dewey, 1899–1924* (Vol. 6, pp. 178–357). Carbondale: Southern Illinois University Press.

Dewey, J. (1916/1972). Democracy and education. In J. A. Boydston (Ed.), *The Later Works of John Dewey, 1925–1953* (Vol. 5, pp. 2–375). Carbondale: Southern Illinois University Press.

Dewey, J. (1920/1972). The sequel of the student revolt. In J. A. Boydston (Ed.), *The Middle Works of John Dewey, 1899–1924* (Vol. 12, pp. 23–28). Carbondale: Southern Illinois University Press.

Dewey, J. (1926/1985). Affective thought. In J. A. Boydston (Ed.), *The Later Works of John Dewey, 1925–1953* (Vol. 2, pp. 105–111). Carbondale: Southern Illinois University Press.

Dewey, J. (1927/1985). The public and its problems. In J. A. Boydston (Ed.), *The Later Works of John Dewey, 1925–1953* (Vol. 2, pp. 236–373). Carbondale: Southern Illinois University Press.

Dewey, J. (1929/1985). Experience and nature. In J. A. Boydston (Ed.), *The Later Works of John Dewey, 1925–1953* (2nd ed., Vol. 1, pp. 2–327). Carbondale: Southern Illinois University Press.

Dewey, J. (1930a/1985). From absolutism to experimentalism. In J. A. Boydston (Ed.), *The Later Works of John Dewey, 1925–1953* (Vol. 5, pp. 148–161). Carbondale: Southern Illinois University Press.

Dewey, J. (1930b/1985). Qualitative thought. In J. A. Boydston (Ed.), *The Later Works of John Dewey, 1925–1953* (Vol. 5, pp. 244–263). Carbondale: Southern Illinois University Press.

Dewey, J. (1933a/1985). Why have progressive schools? In J. A. Boydston (Ed.), *The Later Works of John Dewey, 1925–1953* (Vol. 9, pp. 148–158). Carbondale: Southern Illinois University Press.

Dewey, J. (1933b/1985). How we think. In J. A. Boydston (Ed.), *The Later Works of John Dewey, 1925–1953*. (Rev. ed., Vol. 9, pp. 106–353). Carbondale: Southern Illinois University Press.

Dewey, J. (1934/1985). Art as experience. In J. A. Boydston (Ed.), *The Later Works of John Dewey, 1925–1953* (Vol. 10, pp. 2–353). Carbondale: Southern Illinois University Press.

Dewey, J. (1937/1985). The challenge of democracy to education. In J. A. Boydston (Ed.), *The Later Works of John Dewey, 1925–1953* (Vol. 11, pp. 182–191). Carbondale: Southern Illinois University Press.

Dewey, J. (1938a/1985). Experience and education. In J. A. Boydston (Ed.), *The Later Works of John Dewey, 1925–1953* (Vol. 13, pp. 2–63). Carbondale: Southern Illinois University Press.

Dewey, J. (1938b/1985). Logic: The theory of inquiry. In J. A. Boydston (Ed.), *The Later Works of John Dewey, 1925–1953* (Vol. 12, pp. 2–529). Carbondale: Southern Illinois University Press.

Dewey, J. (1938c/1985). Democracy and education in the world of today. In J. A. Boydston (Ed.), *The Later Works of John Dewey, 1925–1953* (Vol. 13, pp. 295–304). Carbondale: Southern Illinois University Press.

Dewey, J. (1940/1985). Nature in experience. In J. A. Boydston (Ed.), *The Later Works of John Dewey, 1925–1953* (Vol. 14, pp. 142–155). Carbondale: Southern Illinois University Press.

Dewey, J. (1950/1985). Aesthetic experience as a primary phase and as an artistic development. In J. A. Boydston (Ed.), *The Later Works of John Dewey, 1925–1953* (Vol. 16, pp. 396–399). Carbondale: Southern Illinois University Press.

Dewey, J., & Dewey, E. (1915/1972). Schools of tomorrow. In J. A. Boydston (Ed.), *The Middle Works of John Dewey, 1899–1924* (Vol. 8, pp. 206–405). New York, NY: E. P. Dutton & Company.

Elementary school journal. (1916). Educational writings. *The Elementary School Journal, 17*, 13–23.

Kliebard, H. M. (2006). Dewey's reconstruction of the curriculum: From occupation to disciplined knowledge. In D. T. Hansen (Ed.), *John Dewey and Our Educational Prospect* (pp. 113–127). Albany: State University of New York Press.

Labaree, D. F. (2010). How Dewey lost: The victory of David Snedden and social efficiency in the reform of American education. In D. Trohler, T. Schlag, & F. Osterwalder (Eds.), *Pragmatism and modernities* (pp. 163–188). Rotterdam: Sense Publishers.

Quay, J. (2013). *Education, experience and existence: Engaging Dewey, Peirce and Heidegger*. Abingdon: Routledge.

Quay, J. (2015). *Understanding life in school*. New York, NY: Palgrave Macmillan.

Quay, J., & Seaman, J. (2013). *John Dewey and education outdoors*. Rotterdam: Sense Publishers.

Young, E. F. (1916). Democracy and education. *The Journal of Education, 84*, 5–6.

Thinking my way back to you: John Dewey on the communication and formation of concepts

MEGAN J. LAVERTY

Abstract

Contemporary educational theorists focus on the significance of Dewey's conception of experience, learning-by-doing and collateral learning. In this essay, I reexamine the chapters of Dewey's Democracy and Education, *that pertain to thinking and highlight their relationship to Dewey's* How We Think: A Restatement of the Relation of Reflective Thinking in the Educative Process—*another book written explicitly for teachers. In* How We Think *Dewey explains that nothing is more important in education than the formation of concepts. Concepts introduce permanency into an otherwise impermanent world. He defines concepts as established meanings, or intellectual deposits used to found a better understanding of new experiences; they are what makes any experience educationally worthwhile. Dewey accuses traditional and progressive education of failing to appropriately form concepts in students. His position is that concepts are formed and transformed by experience, reflection and activity. He argues that the individual makes a personalized use of concepts for which he or she requires: continuity of experience, exposure to new or surprising possibilities, and sustained communication with others—all of which are discussed at length in* Democracy & Education. *I conclude with the practical recommendation that K-12 schools introduce philosophy into the curriculum. Philosophy not only invites students to engage their concepts in a reflective manner, but it also provides a valuable resource for that engagement. Most if not all of philosophy's canonical texts are dedicated to analyzing such concepts as beauty, friendship, love and justice. The introduction of philosophy in K-12 education would, I suggest, offer a correction to both traditional and progressive education.*

> Thinking about events and celebrating them in tone and color and form might become more important than being an event.
>
> *John Dewey*[1]

JOHN DEWEY'S DEMOCRACY AND EDUCATION IN AN ERA OF GLOBALIZATION

Introduction: Thinking matters

Why focus on thinking in a special issue dedicated to the centenary of John Dewey's *Democracy and Education*? Thinking figures in *Democracy and Education*, but not prominently. It is referenced in two chapters: 'Experience and Thinking' and 'Thinking in Education'. These chapters appear in the middle section of the book (Chapters 8–14), which represents matters that David T. Hansen identifies as 'resid[ing] at the heart of teaching and learning: aims, motivation, interest, self-discipline, social interaction, thinking, method, subject and more' (2006, p. 11). As thinking is only one factor among many, educators can overlook it as they focus upon other educational issues, such as motivation, interest, and social interaction. Moreover, as Dewey acknowledges, these chapters dwell on the negative: they explain, for example, that mental busy-work does *not* qualify as thinking. In a little-known essay entitled, 'The Teacher in John Dewey's Works', however, Maxine Greene interprets *Democracy and Education* as establishing the premise that '[t]he end in view [of deliberate or conscious teaching] is the effectual development of thought, along with the enrichment of experience to which this would lead' (1989, p. 28). In line with Greene's assessment, I will endeavor to explain what the effectual development of thought consists in and why, now more than ever, it is important that young people exercise conceptual agency.

The educational potency of Dewey's theory of concepts has yet to be appreciated. The debate between traditional and progressive educators, which was chiefly organized around their pedagogical differences, eclipsed Dewey's central point about the effectual development of thought. Progressive education is a broad theoretical and practical approach to elementary and secondary schooling (K-12). It came to prominence in the US during the nineteenth century, dominated the early part of the twentieth century, and receded in the late 1950s. It defined itself in opposition to the scholasticism of traditional schooling. Despite Dewey's efforts to disassociate himself from progressive education and what he saw as its misappropriation of his ideas, his name remains associated with it.

Dewey articulated many of the concerns that acted as catalysts for the emergence and popularity of progressive education. He argued that the subject matter of traditional schooling 'easily becomes remote and dead—abstract and bookish', and that it is isolated from the dynamism and change of life experience (MW 9: 11). He wrote: 'We get so thoroughly used to a kind of pseudo-idea, a half-perception, that we are not aware of how half-dead our mental action is' (MW 9: 150). In other words, students only appear to be thinking because they have nothing to do mentally. One strategy for inciting thinking, recommended by both Dewey and William Heard Kilpatrick, is to involve students in purposeful activities that 'suggest and prepare for succeeding activities' (Kilpatrick, 1918, p. 12).[2] Kilpatrick argued that the successive nature of the activities ensure 'that the individual has been modified so that he sees what before he did not see or does what before he could not do. But this is exactly to say that the activity has had an educative effect' (Kilpatrick, 1918, p. 12). The 'project method' proved to be such an accessible and powerful idea that it entered educational terminology and contributed to the progressive focus on spontaneous and wholehearted activity.

Having conceived of education in terms of practical activity, progressive educators sought to disavow self-consciously intellectual pursuits.[3] Dewey thought this position deeply flawed and potentially miseducative, however. While he valued the progressive turn to psychology, he remained critical of its failure to move experience in the direction of its logical order. According to Dewey, no experience is educative unless it tends towards greater understanding and a more orderly arrangement of that understanding. He thought that progressive educators had failed to appreciate his endorsement of the traditional focus on concept formation. In *How We Think: A Restatement of the Relation of Reflective Thinking to the Educative Process*,[4]—a book written specifically for teachers—he stresses that: 'With respect to teaching there is no more important topic than the question of the way in which genuine concepts are formed' (LW 8: 240). He also thought that traditional educators had sidestepped the question by assuming that concepts were to be acquired 'in accord with the logical grammar of particular subjects' (Greene 1989, p. 27; Hirst, 1967, p. 50). He argued that the logical order is insufficient for the development of thought because it prevents concepts from gaining purchase in students' minds; students do not know how to use these concepts, which effectively reduces concepts to 'mere words and empty symbolisms' (Greene 1989, p. 29).

Put differently, traditional education forms *nominal* as opposed to *genuine* concepts: nominal concepts are remote from experience and incapable of modifying apprehension, whereas genuine concepts are the intellectual deposits of experience and which modify apprehension, understanding, and behavior. Progressive educators underestimated Dewey's regard for the traditional focus on conceptual understanding and missed the intended target of his critique: the traditional theory of concepts which assumes that concepts standardize what we know and are acquired by a means 'of induction, that is extraction of a common meaning from several "ready-made" objects' (Hickman, 2011, p. 198). By implication, concepts are acquired 'ready-made from some external source'; and once acquired, they need only be applied (Hickman, 2011, p. 196).

By contrast, while Dewey accepts that concepts introduce permanency into an otherwise impermanent world, he insists that concepts are formed and transformed by experience, reflection, and activity. As Thomas A. Alexander explains, Dewey understands 'thinking—thinking not thought—as a process in the lifeworld and not its underpinning' (Alexander, 2014). Thus, for Dewey, thinking is 'the consummate act of human freedom' (Jackson, 2012). Concepts are never completely fixed or finished (Hickman, 2011, p. 198). Dewey writes that '[t]he great reward of exercising the power of thinking is that there are no limits to the possibility of carrying over into the objects and events of life, meaning originally acquired by thoughtful examination and hence no limit to the continual growth of meaning in human life' (LW 8: 128). Dewey's account 'emphasizes expansion of significance and meaning by means of experimentation, rather than assembling, categorizing, and referring' (Hickman, 2011, p. 198). In *Democracy and Education*, Dewey argues that the individual makes a personalized use of the concepts he or she requires according to her continuity of experience, exposure to new or surprising possibilities, and sustained communication with others.

In what follows, I explain why the call to think, that is, to enrich meaning and exercise freedom, is so pressing in today's globalized world. Then I elucidate how Dewey's philosophy of communication draws from his theories of language and meaning. In conclusion, I consider Philosophy for/with Children as an example of how contemporary educators might teach reflective thinking.

Free and open communication in a globalized world

Dewey visited China, Japan, Turkey, South Africa, and Mexico, among other places, at a time when such travel was arduous by today's standards. He used these opportunities to explore varieties of education scarcely known in the United States at the time. Dewey believed this exposure to be important (Gaudelli & Laverty, 2015; Hansen, 2009b; Saito, 2006). He never wavered in his commitment to the democratic way of life (Saito, 2006, p. 136). In *Democracy and Education*, he endeavors to apply democratic ideals to education, suggesting that society in the US is only 'nominally democratic' (MW 9: 3). He understood that we cannot assume either that democracy is uniquely American or that it will perpetuate itself automatically. His letters from China and Japan reveal that he thought that citizens of the US had much to learn from other cultures. According to Dewey, democracy is a moral ideal that requires 'the creation of personal attitudes in human beings' (LW 14: 226). These attitudes could be described as convictions or articles of faith. They include: a belief in others' capacity for intelligent judgment and action; a commitment to working together; and the recognition that the process of experience is educative.

Only an education that permits free and full communication will instill these personal attitudes. The value of free and full communication is that it allows for the 'the give and take of ideas, facts, experiences,' and offers 'differences a chance to show themselves' (LW 14: 228). Anything short of free and full communication will set 'up barriers that divide human beings into sets and cliques, into antagonistic sects and factions' (LW 4: 227). As Dewey foresaw, globalization offers heretofore unsurpassed opportunities for free and open communication on a previously unimaginable scale, with the constant development of transportation, information, and communication technologies, people can be in almost constant contact with one another. They can engage in long-distance cultural exchanges and artistic collaborations; they can develop communities that bridge every manner of divide; and they can organize and attend world summits on climate change. There can be no doubt that globalization has accelerated the circulation of goods, information, and people, and resulted in our almost unlimited access to diverse histories, religions, and cultures (Papastephanou, 2005, p. 543; Rizvi & Lingard, 2000, p. 419).

The world is becoming a community of nations, with increased international trade, travel, and immigration, and the development of new information technologies. These technologies have dramatically altered how individuals communicate. For example, a professor can reside in Europe, be employed by an American University, and teach international students via the internet. As this example demonstrates, geographical proximity is no longer necessary for free and full communication. Our social relations have a global reach. In turn, globalization has become an integral dimension of everyday life. As Anthony Giddens (1990) observes 'local events are shaped by events occurring many miles away and vice versa' (p. 64).

Yet other scholars, including Patrick Fitzsimons (2000), Hansen (2009a), Bruce Haynes (2002), Kathy Hytten (2009) and Mariana Papastephanou (2005) caution that we should not be naively optimistic as the current unprecedented interdependence of nations making up the global community provides similarly unprecedented opportunities for exploitation, consumerism, and greed. Globalization is contributing to the widening and deepening of inequity. Traditional ways of living are becoming precarious. Individuals report feeling disintegrated, displaced, and disaffected as they experience the erosion of the rituals and customs which register the meaningfulness of their experience. In theory, our increased interdependence should make it easier for individuals across the globe to consider the well-being of all. Globalization presents its own obstacles to realizing this well-being, however.

Globalization has contributed to rising numbers of migrants and refugees who seek asylum from political, ethnic, and religious fundamentalism. The expansion of immigration, complemented by the threat of terrorism, has created new challenges that, to quote Naoko Saito, 'necessitate us to consider the meaning of citizenship, not only within a national boundary, but also beyond it on a global scale' (Saito, 2006, p. 133). It is not surprising that we experience globalization as a complex, empirical phenomenon to which we are subject rather than as a result of what we do (Papastephanou, 2005, p. 534). In the flurry of informational exchange and communicative activity, individuals find themselves seeking guidance on how to live. Islam and Buddhism are the fastest growing religions, yoga and meditation classes are proliferating, and the 'self-help' sections of bookstores have ballooned in recent years. The search is an urgent one: without guidance, the perils we face are increasingly sinister. Educators report being concerned about child obesity, consumerism, and teenage suicide. It is as if the tools and instruments upon which we once depended to navigate the world have become antiquated.

One explanation is that feeling figuratively adrift in the world today disguises 'a deep and unreflective rootedness in the Occidental culture of performativity, modernization and profit' (Papastephanou, 2005, p. 542). In other words, economic globalization is synonymous with the imposition of 'a single dominant culture as the model of all operations' (Papastephanou, 2005, p. 536). This unilateral, competitive culture has lead to increasing modernization (Papastephanou, 2005, p. 542), a revival of neoliberalism (Papastephanou, 2005, p. 543), the standardization of taste (Saito, 2006, p. 131), and the treatment of education as a means to national ends (Haynes, 2002; Heath, 2002, p. 38; Papastephanou, 2005, p. 544).

Another explanation for this endemic rootlessness is that economic, scientific, technological, and political change is so rapid that it is hard for individuals to meaningfully assimilate them. If, as Dewey thought, new experiences are mediated by meanings gathered from past experiences, then we need time for the slow accretion of meanings. That is, we need time to test new ideas. New ideas may be vague initially but are refined through a process of experimentation enacted through behavioral responses. For Dewey, experience is not primarily a feature of an individual's subjective awareness. Rather, it is social and historical; passed from one generation to the next, and it provides the formative context for individuals. Other terms that Dewey uses to describe experience include 'mind' and 'culture'. It is culture that 'allows us to participate in a shared life of meaning and value; it is the basis for our having a sense of self and sense of other'. (Alexander, 2014, p. 82). Thus, most judgments, thoughts, and reflections are based on habits formed in the give-and-take of relationships constitutive of a culture. With globalization, however, the nature of these relationships, and thus the forms of these habits, are being altered at such a rapid rate, that culture no longer provides us with the same ground and contextualization.

The problem is compounded by the fact that globalization has ushered in 'a moment of extreme technicist concern' (Greene 1989, p. 28). Problem-solving, which Dewey proposed as a model for thinking, is 'largely defined in terms of means-ends relations' (Greene 1989, p. 28). In other words, thinking becomes 'all about "achieving outcomes" more quickly, more often and more effectively than before'. (Heath, 2002, p. 38). Defined as procedural or instrumental, thinking is associated with innovation, productivity, and efficiency. Gone is the emphasis on critical reflection, enlightenment, and conceptual understanding. Technicist thinking represents a misinterpretation of Dewey, for although he emphasized the practical benefits of thinking—namely that it delivers us from problematic situations—he stressed that it enriches the meaning of ordinary experience.

The meaningful assimilation of new experiences is critical for growth. The danger of globalization is that it contributes to the formation of nominal concepts, which are incapable of performing truly useful work. To quote Greene, 'mere words and empty symbolisms are not sufficient when it comes to the development of thought' (1989, p. 29). If concepts are to be genuine, they must factor within a process. According to Dewey, if individuals fail to grow, then dogmatism and dissipation set in. Only by thinking can we 'rebuild the spirit of common understanding, of mutual sympathy and goodwill among all people's and races' (LW 9: 203). What is needed then to re-establish the importance of genuine concepts in the face of such unprecedented changes? Dewey's philosophy of language offers some answers to this question.

Dewey's philosophy of language

It is customary to assume that our relevant conceptual capacities are discursive in nature. This leads us to overlook Dewey's theory of concept formation as his philosophy is focused on experience rather than language. It is worth noting, even at the risk of over-simplification, that a debate is underway in the philosophical literature between those who endorse the classical pragmatists as rightly focused on experience, on the one hand, and linguistic or neo-pragmatists as Richard Rorty, Robert Brandom, and Cheryl Misak, on the other, who prefer to focus exclusively on language without recourse to experience. In addition, some philosophers—Richard Bernstein, Jean Pierre Cometti, and Steven Levine, for example—identify Dewey as having already made the linguistic turn (Dreon, 2009, p. 11). Together, they offer readings that seek to 'recover and develop broadly Deweyan, classical pragmatist conceptions of experience while being able to respect, having thus broadened, the pragmatic tradition's requirements on meaning and rational intelligibility' (O'Shea, p. 58). As James R. Shea explains, according to this view, concepts 'embody implicit hypotheses in relation to the course of future experience and action, so reflected in our commitments in practice to the corresponding patterns of inference and action' (O'Shea, p. 41).

Dewey conceives of language as communication. He considers it what Thomas A. Alexander describes as a 'world of mutual symbolic participation, of *shared experience*' (Alexander, 2014; p. 66). It is the 'communicative, conversational structure of language' that forces individuals to move away from themselves (Dreon, 2009, p. 112). They imagine the other's perspective as they are imaginatively called to see themselves from another's perspective (Alexander, 2014, p. 66; Dreon, 2009, p. 112). If language is 'an interactive process of symbolic communication involving mutual imaginative copresence', then concepts animate more than linguistic propositions (Alexander, 2014, p. 66); they are revealed in 'spontaneous gestures, music, painting, dance, architecture and ritual practices' (Johnson, 2009, p. 18). Thus, Dewey's philosophy of language encompasses the rich plurality of human experience. From his perspective, it is 'the full symbolic mode of human existence'; 'human existence is *inherently* cultural co-existence' (Alexander, 2014, p.84).

In *Experience and Nature,* Dewey enlists religious terminology to describe communication as follows:

> Of all affairs, communication is the most wonderful. That things should be able to pass from the plane of external pushing and pulling to that of revealing themselves to man, and thereby to themselves; and that the fruit of communication should be participation, sharing, is a wonder by the side of which transubstantiation pales. (Dewey LW 1: 132)

For those unfamiliar with Roman Catholic theological doctrine, the sacrament of transubstantiation is performed by an ordained priest, who converts the bread and wine into the body and blood of Jesus Christ. The conversion is considered metaphysical: Roman Catholics believe that the consecrated bread and wine are sacred because Jesus Christ is literally present 'in' them. The point of Dewey's comparison is to suggest that communication involves a metaphysical conversion that is even more miraculous. According to him, the conversion that takes place in communication is, to quote Dewey, 'ultimately worthy of awe, admiration and loyal appreciation' (Dewey LW 1: 132).

Communication converts existence into experience. The 'signs and symbols' that are the means of communication—'gestures, pictures, monuments, visual images, finger movements'—do not simply represent the elements of experience; rather, they *create* experience by converting the senseless push and pull of qualitative immediacies into meanings or objects of thoughts (LW 2: 371; MW 6: 314). This conversion is a form of communion because meanings or objects of thought, unlike qualitative immediacies, are uniquely shared. According to Dewey, 'events cannot be passed from one to another, but meanings may be shared by means of signs' (LW2: 331). The view that meanings, and not events, are shared might appear counter-intuitive: common sense tells us that language describes and therefore comes *after* shared human experience, and that language sometimes impedes individuals' ability to share an experience. According to Dewey, however, events cannot be shared because they cannot be thought. They exist on 'the plane of external pushing and pulling' (LW 1: 132). To be without language is to be submerged in a 'rapid and roaring stream of events' (LW 1: 132). Although sensory immediacies can be qualitatively differentiated, they remain 'dumbly rapturous' (LW 1: 132). It is only language that transforms this senseless flow into events, and parses it into objects of experience and thought, that is into things with meaning. As the objects of thought, events 'become capable of survey, contemplation and ideal, or logical observation' (LW 1: 133). In summary, it is not that our 'conceptual capacities are exercised on non-conceptual deliverances of sensibility', but rather that 'conceptual capacities are already operative in the deliverances of sensibility themselves' (McDowell, 1996, p. 39).

Communication is instrumental for all forms of human engagement, ranging from the mundane to the accomplished. It follows, therefore, that the better our communication, the greater our capacity to effectively cooperate in the service of mutual interests. Dewey cautions against focusing exclusively on the instrumental function of communication because the scope of individuals' activities is too limited to exhaust the role of language in the formation of genuine concepts. We must also recognize what Dewey terms the 'final' function of communication which is to expand, enhance, solidify, and deepen their shared meanings. The final function of communication holds an 'intrinsic delight' or 'inhering fascination': we feel momentarily 'detached from immediate instrumental consequences of assistance and cooperative action' (LW 1: 158). Focusing exclusively on the final function of communication, however, is 'luxurious and corrupting for some; brutal, trivial, harsh for others' (LW 1: 160). Thus, Dewey concludes, that the aim is to balance the instrumental and final functions of communication.

The ideas of balance and rhythm are central to Dewey's thought. Dewey defines rhythm as the 'ordered variation of changes' or 'rationality among qualities' (LW 10: 158, 174). He conceives of it as the 'universal scheme of existence, underlying all realization of order in change' (LW 10: 154). Rhythm divides existence into measures that allow for variation in emphasis and intensity. If there is 'order, rhythm and balance', then it 'means that energies significant for experience are acting at their best' (LW 10: 189). His account of rhythm highlights the fact that in most communication, for practical reasons, a common background 'is silently sup-plied and im-plied as the taken-for granted medium' (LW 8: 342). It is for essentially practical reasons that individuals grasp the meanings of words. Fixed by the concrete underpinnings of practical life, these meanings encourage individuals to behave as if words were defined by such material entities as clothes, cars, houses, schools, and neighborhoods (LW 8: 294–295).

In daily life, it is impractical to 'dig up' and formulate the common background that we take for granted in our communications. If we were to inspect this background, however, we would find gaps, impasses, and ruptures. These fissures are inevitable: we cannot eliminate indefiniteness of meaning from our conventional understanding of words. We get ideas from experience, and because 'experience is not a rigid and closed thing' but rather 'vital and hence growing', it is impossible to predict the 'increment[s] of meaning' that accrue as we proceed (LW 8:277). The inevitability and uncertainty of the meaning-making process is dramatized in our vulnerability to misunderstanding. In the case of a misunderstanding, the individuals involved must review the taken-for-granted in an effort to disclose 'what was unconsciously assumed' (LW 8: 342). This investigative process is an essential feature of communication.

The case of the child's acquisition of language is another dramatization of how experience sculpts meaning. This is well illustrated by Dewey's example of the child who begins with whatever significance he can extract from his interactions with the family dog. What he discerns shapes his expectations and behavior, as he eagerly tries to apply the concept to each new experience. It becomes, Dewey explains, 'a working tool of further apprehensions, an instrument of understanding other things' (LW 8:242). In Dewey's example, the boy anticipates that the next 'dog'—which turns out to be a horse—will be furry, friendly, four-legged, and brown. He revises his understanding in light of his encounter with the horse because he is attuned to the fact that his concepts are no more than hypotheses. For this reason, they are always open to development through use. Dewey concludes that '[i]n learning to understand and make words, children learn more than the words themselves. They gain a habit that opens a new world to them' (LW 8: 283).

As individuals age, however, and their lives become more settled, their eagerness to be estranged from their own world—to discover new perspectives—perishes. Adults, unlike the child in Dewey's example, are subject to the tyranny of habit, custom, and routine. Thus, their aversion to estrangement is unsurprising. Dewey believes, however, that adults can and should resist the interpretive inertia. He urges individuals not to allow their utterances to proceed 'on a superficial and trivial plane' by assuming that all meanings are stable and satisfactorily given (LW 2: 349). While communication requires a certain standardization to stabilize meaning, this agreement is vulnerable owing to the deep differences in experience and understanding that persist. And it is, at times, the recognition of those differences that can shift perspective. Thus, unfamiliarity, the source of our misunderstandings, is as foundational to thought and communication as familiarity. As Dewey explains, 'experience may welcome and assimilate all that the most exact penetrating thought discovers', and even the most mundane objects, activities, and relationships can be seen in a new light, opening 'new vistas of experience' (LW 8: 277–278).

Full and complete meaning is as elusive as full and complete mutual understanding. As humans, we cannot know all there is to know about being human. And yet, we do not find ourselves more enlightened by 'moving beyond' our ordinarily practical lives. Rather than directing us to speak outside our ordinary use of language and the assumptions which give our communication force, Dewey encourages us to recognize something we already know, namely that by engaging more fully in life, we widen our range of acquaintance with people, practices, and things. This enables us to discover new and unforeseen possibilities, to deepen our conceptual understandings and to extend our responsibility.

Speaking a language is a creative endeavor, that is, to quote Murdoch, 'something progressive, something infinitely perfectible' (1970, p. 23). We are without rules or guidelines, and yet the possibility of communication is at stake. Communication is participatory, in the sense that it makes something common 'in at least two different centers of behavior' (LW 1: 141). In other words, meaning is never wholly in the mind, but unfolds *in* and *with* others. Dewey explains this point as follows: 'Various phases of participation by one in another's joys, sorrows, sentiments and purposes, are distinguished by the scope and depth of the objects that are held in common, from a momentary caress to continued insight and loyalty' (LW 1: 158). Thus, he concludes that it is by means of understanding the common things—'a flower, a gleam of moonlight, the song of a bird'—that our 'lives reach a deeper level' (LW 2:349).

Dewey's conclusion is puzzling. The phenomenology of picking a flower, noticing the moon, or listening to a bird, does not feel particularly special or profound. Dewey denies that words are just tools; rather, he claims that it is an entire way of life that makes 'flowers', 'gleams', 'moonbeams', 'songs', 'birds' possibilities for us. It is helpful at this point to consider an example. Anthony has lived in the same town for 15 years and over this time he regularly visited the local park. Before marriage and children, he would run in the park; he felt a sense of kinship with the other runners. With the arrival of his children, Anthony spent more time in the playground and playing fields; he became friendly with other families. In time, his family bought a dog; they became familiar with the other dog owners and their breeds. As his children grew into adults, they stopped going to the park; Anthony would often walk the dog alone. By this point, the park was replete with meaning.

Over time, the meaning of the common things—kites, dogs, toys, trees—betray their qualitative differences. Although Anthony has the language with which to understand his reality, it is the sum of his experiences that make that language truly meaningful (Dreon, 2009, p. 115). His experiences in the park are configured by a range of shared activities: running, parenting, encouraging, reprimanding, cheering, meeting people, chatting, and walking the dog. Over time, his sense of the common things becomes infused by an understanding of how variously they figure in human life: the disappointment of losing a kite to a tree; frustration with a fussy child; awareness of an aging body; and anxiety when the dog slips its leash. This example highlights the virtuous circle inherent in Dewey's philosophy: 'language contributes to configuring our human way of life, but conversely it is precisely this way of life that makes language meaningful' (Dreon, 2009, p. 115). In his view, meaning, language, communication, and experience are all mutually supporting.

Dewey's insistence upon defining communication as a universal *and* commonplace activity that redeems us through communion reflects his profoundly democratic impulse. Nevertheless, it is naive to think that the adoption of Dewey's philosophy of communication would secure peaceful coexistence, and unrealistic to expect individuals to learn from all experiences, no matter how tiresome, offensive, or hurtful (Biesta, 2006, p. 36; Hansen, 2006). Dewey's thesis stands nonetheless: the more deeply an individual understands a concept, the greater his or her capacity to appreciate its significance in others' lives. It is no surprise that he should think that there is nothing more important in education than the formation of concepts. Concepts, which he defines as established meanings, introduce permanency into an otherwise impermanent world. They are intellectual deposits foundational to understanding new experiences; they make experiences educationally worthwhile. Dewey assumes that the individual actively engaged in making sense of his or her experiences, that is, in concept formation, is susceptible to misunderstanding. For this reason, he stresses that our living and being in the world is experimental and inclined toward fallibilism. The trial and error of the scientific method is not to be viewed as a rigidly formulaic series of steps imposed on experience. Rather, it is naturally embedded in our language and language acquisition. While it is inevitable that individuals will take up language in various ways, even dramatically different ways of speaking and living are embodiments of universally shared concerns.

Dewey argues that both traditional *and* progressive education fail to stimulate students to form concepts. In response, I will conclude with the practical recommendation that K-12 schools introduce philosophy into the curriculum to aid with concept formation. Most canonical philosophical texts are dedicated to analyzing concepts, including beauty, friendship, love, and justice. The practice of philosophical inquiry invites students to engage their own concepts in a reflective manner. I recommend the pre-college training of thought. Ironically, while Dewey is himself recognized as an influential figure for the Philosophy for/with Children Movement, he did not recommend introducing philosophy into the K-12 curriculum (Gregory & Granger, 2012, p. 7; Nussbaum, 2010, p. 73).[5] The movement's founder, Matthew Lipman, speculates that Dewey's reticence is due to his observation that philosophers of education were wary of schools. He writes: 'No, the philosophers of education, Dewey must have concluded, neither would nor could involve their beautiful discipline in the noisy turmoil of the schools'. (1994, p. 148). Lipman may well be right.

Another plausible thesis, however, is that Dewey was concerned that teachers would not grasp that philosophy is intrinsic to experience, language, and culture (LW 3: 3). That is, they would discourage students from conceiving of philosophy as continuous with their own thinking. This worried him because if philosophy was to play a useful role in young people's lives, then it must be grounded in their awareness of cultural context and personal history. He considered the task of philosophy to be 'the critique of prejudices' (LW 1: 40). Yet, as Maughn Gregory and David Granger point out, 'prejudices are, by definition, blind spots. To critique our own cultural or personal prejudices would require us to observe them from a perspective that does not incorporate them' (Gregory & Granger, 2012, p. 5). Dewey suspected, rightly in my view, that pre-college philosophy would repress the continuity in the interest of establishing an academically rigorous subject.

Philosophy for/with Children has sought to resist the urge to repress ordinary life experience.[6] This may explain why Dewey proved to be such an influential figure for the movement (Bleazby, 2011; Cam, 1994; Gregory, 2000; Johnson, 1995; Lipman, 1994; Lipman & Sharp, 1978). Philosophical inquiry begins with a problem, question, or doubt that has arisen within the context of the children's lives. By engaging in inclusive and reasonable dialog, children can experiment with new ways of thinking about it. They draw from the philosophical tradition adapted from their existential context. Together, the tradition, community, and experimentation enable them to respond intelligently to a problem, question, or doubt. It becomes an occasion for meaning-making, as the psychological origins of thinking take on, with time, a more logical order and the gap between the psychological and the logical is gradually closed (Gregory & Granger, 2012, p. 16).

Dewey and philosophy for/with children

Philosophy for/with Children is an international movement organized around the teaching of pre-college philosophy. It originated a little over 40 years ago when Lipman designed a curriculum, based on his novel *Harry Stottlemeier's Discovery*, intended to expose young adolescents to the central concepts and principles of philosophy. Influenced by American pragmatism, Lipman conceived of philosophy as an endeavor of collective inquiry, beginning with problematic experiences, and leading toward warranted judgments. In *Harry Stottlemeier's Discovery*, a group of school-age children discover the principles of basic Aristotelian logic as they consider issues of importance to them including: sibling rivalry, friendship groups, schools, nationalism, and family obligations. Lipman designed *Harry Stottlemeier's Discovery* to stimulate students' dialogical inquiry, under the guidance of a teacher with sufficient philosophical expertise to draw out the themes and arguments of the text, and encourage the students as they learned to philosophize.

The early success of Lipman's novel challenged the view that philosophy is a demanding and esoteric field of study reserved for university students. No one had thought to engage children in philosophical inquiry since it was widely assumed that they were incapable of it and that it was an inappropriate activity for childhood (which amounted to the same thing). Children were viewed as insufficiently rational, impulsive, lacking in self-awareness, and erratic in their familial relationships. They could move from extreme frustration to delirious excitement in a matter of minutes. With his philosophical curriculum, however, Lipman revealed that our conceptions of both children and philosophy were impoverished. Although children might lack life experience, we must trust that their engagement with it is as searching and dynamic as that of an adult, sometimes more so.

Perhaps the most striking feature of Ann Margaret Sharp and Lipman's curriculum[7] is its profound trust in our everyday responses and the ordinary language in which those responses are articulated. The appropriate understanding of the meaning of a word is established through a process of discovery and invention. An individual must take responsibility for how she uses a word, and reflect on that use with respect to both her past experiences and others' use of that word. Without a final arbiter, individuals are condemned to persuade and re-persuade one another of the correct way to proceed with language. This insight itself is not new; what *is* new is Lipman's application of it to the education of children and adolescents. The community of philosophical inquiry, the pedagogical signature of P4C, involves individuals speaking, thinking, and being together in an effort to discover their meaning and bring it alive for others.

Pre-college philosophy differs from its university counterpart (Laverty, 2014a). It is less reliant on knowledge of the philosophical tradition and involves greater consideration of how experiences, stories, and images crystallize a way of thinking and an orientation to life. It is reliant upon the children's powers of description and imagination, as they seek to suspend their own understanding and commitments in an effort to recognize and appreciate alternative world views. It entails a willingness to self-correct in light of better understanding. These are key tenets in the ever-expanding and diversifying philosophy-in-schools movement.

When I think of children in philosophical conversation, I imagine a classroom of small individuals sitting around in a circle, looking back and forth at one another and earnestly listening to what each has to say. I hear them contesting such concepts as 'friendship' or 'fairness', asking for reasons, reiterating what has been said in the interests of clarification, offering experiences from their own lives to serve as examples and counter-examples, and proposing hypothetical solutions. I see thinking in their faces, their expression of delight and surprise on hearing another's idea, quiet wondering, laughter, and the alternatively authoritative and playful ways they express themselves by straightening and twisting their bodies. Finally, I imagine children gaging the development of their own intellectual community, by evaluating the relevance of their discussion, and determining whether everyone spoke, practiced good thinking, and advanced their understanding.

Philosophical conversation with children frequently focuses on a theme. Students may dedicate an entire semester to reading and analyzing stories about friendship, for example, developing and testing criteria, and probing related issues of loyalty, betrayal, and trust. Each child is challenged to take responsibility for what he or she means by 'friend', and to see himself or herself as united with others in this endeavor. These discussions provide opportunities for children to exercise their intellectual autonomy in concert with others; their thinking is informed by reflection on experience *and* discussion with peers. Each individual must work out for herself or himself what it is that *we* mean by friendship; the 'for herself/for himself' and the 'we' are equally important.

Philosophical conversation is a means of individual and collective meaning-making. It invites children to share, contest, and deepen their concepts. We learn from Dewey that language-users, including very young children, are the recipients *and* producers of meaning. While a child's conceptual understanding is shaped by the cultural and linguistic practices of the community to which he belongs, he can creatively engage with this inheritance by encountering individuals from different communities as they seek to determine the true meanings of concepts. This process enables children to trace the sources of their concepts to parental, cultural, and religious, authorities. It also demonstrates that concepts are never finalized, which means that each and every individual must *learn* his or her concepts. The inevitability of our conceptual learning requires us to be in communication with one another, no matter how different or opposed we feel ourselves to be.

If we withhold children from the possibility of philosophical engagement, we deprive them of an intellectual, esthetic, and ethical—that is, an *educational*—good. It is an intellectual good because the children are engaged in philosophical inquiry with reference to their own experience, which utilizes all of their mental resources in a concerted effort to extend their understanding and overturn misconceptions. Philosophy with children is an esthetic good in virtue of its beauty. It is beautiful to see, and be with, people ruminating together on life's big questions in an effort to take greater responsibility for their lives, and there is beauty in the symphony of different voices, the rhythmic contrast between sound and silence, the ebb and flow of intensity, and the interweaving of the different thematic concerns. Finally, the invitation, from adults to children, to philosophize is an ethical good by way of its symbolic and performative function. It identifies, at the same time as it contributes to, the common humanity of children, acknowledging them as members of the ethical community as it invites them to be a part of it. For, to philosophize with children is to assume that the child is neither a partial, nor exceptional, human being; rather, children, like adults, are endeavoring to live better, more meaningful lives, with the potential for wisdom, and the ability to shape and educate our 'adult' understanding of how to live better.

A concluding remark on Dewey's educational legacy

It has been one hundred years since the publication of Dewey's *Democracy and Education*. This text still has much to offer us, particularly as our world faces similarly dramatic changes to those Dewey's generation experienced. The task of democracy—'creation of a freer and more humane experience in which all share and to which all contribute'—still confronts us (LW 4: 230). My goal has been to highlight the value of Dewey's commitment to the importance of reflective thought in school education. It gives individual children voices, allowing their differences to be revealed. Educators inevitably enlist ideas, but those committed to thinking will invite children and adolescents to speak for themselves. This, in turn, will create opportunities for children's and adolescents' concepts to be articulated, challenged, and refined. Dewey sums it up as follows:

> We can and do supply ready-made 'ideas' by the thousand; we do not usually take much pains to see that the one learning engages in significant situations where his own activities generate, support and clinch ideas—that is, perceived meanings or connections. This does not mean that the teacher is to stand off and look on; the alternative to furnishing ready-made subject matter and listening to the accuracy with which it is reproduced is not quiescence, but participation, sharing, in an activity. In such shared activity, the teacher is a learner, and the learner is, without knowing it, a teacher—and upon the whole, the less consciousness there is, on either side, of either giving or receiving instruction, the better. (MW 9: 167)

Dewey holds that educators should recognize that they dwell within the paradox of our humanity. They should seek to involve their students in experiences that will expand the meaningfulness and efficaciousness of their future experiences. Yet, they must vigilantly guard against conceptual totalitarianism.

Acknowledgements

I am grateful to Tomas Rocha for his gracious, timely and expert research assistance. Thanks to Diana Barnes, Andrea English, Mordechai Gordon, Rachel Longa and two anonymous reviewers for their invaluable feedback on an earlier version of this article.

Disclosure statement

No potential conflict of interest was reported by the author.

Notes

1. John Dewey (1988b). Hereafter the *Middle Works* are abbreviated as MS and the *Later Works* are abbreviated as LW.
2. Kilpatrick was later blamed for encouraging anti-intellectualism among classroom teachers. Lawrence Cremin argued that 'in seeking to make Dewey's ideas manageable for mass consumption by the teaching profession', Kilpatrick had 'ended up by transforming them into versions quite different from the originals' (Cremin, 1964, p. 221).
3. Contemporary educational theorists have continued to overlook Dewey's commitment to reflective thinking. While texts such as *The Child and the Curriculum*, *My Pedagogic Creed*, *Experience and Education* and *Democracy and Education* are regularly taught in pre-service and in-service education courses, teachers are rarely exposed to *How We Think*, despite the fact that it was written specifically for teachers.
4. There are two editions of *How We Think*: the first was published in 1910 (six years before the publication of *Democracy and Education* in 1916) and the second in 1933. Only the second edition includes the subtitle, *A Restatement of the Relation of Reflective Thinking to the Educative Process*, perhaps indicating Dewey's sense of himself as having failed to adequately emphasize the role of reflective thinking in the educative process.
5. For more on the relationship of Dewey's thought to children's philosophical practice, see the special issue of *Education and Culture* (2012), guest edited by Maughn Gregory. Contributors include: Eric Anthamatten, Jennifer B. Bleazby, David Kennedy, Nadia Stoyanova Kennedy, Stefano Oliverio and Mark D. Tschaepe. Also see Stephanie Burdick-Shepherd's dissertation entitled, 'Reading for Childhood in Philosophy and Literature: An Ethical Practice for Educators.'
6. As Gregory and Granger point out in their introduction to the special issue of Education and Culture on the relationship of Dewey's thought to children's philosophical practice: 'In current programmatic and research literature phrases such as, "Philosophy for Children," "Philosophy With Children and Adolescents," "Philosophy in Schools," and "Philosophy for Young People," are used interchangeably to refer to any program that engages children in philosophical dialog—as opposed, especially, to high school courses in which philosophy is studied as an academic subject' (Gregory & Granger, 2012, footnote 6, pp. 24–25).
7. In 1974, Matthew Lipman, together with Ann Margaret Sharp, established the Institute for the Advancement of Philosophy for Children (IAPC) at Montclair State University. The two worked tirelessly to develop new materials for younger and older children, disseminate the program in many countries around the world, and build up a cadre of experienced teachers and teacher trainers. To quote Gregory & Granger, 'Lipman and Sharp's was the first systematic approach to pre-college philosophy education, including a theorized curriculum and pedagogy' (Gregory & Granger, 2012, p. 6). With the international expansion of Philosophy for Children, practitioners in a variety of national and cultural settings have adapted Lipman's original model to fit their own contexts while striving to retain its central elements. This reflects a growing maturity and depth which is characteristic of a discipline—in this case, pre-college philosophy—as it grows beyond the initial vision of its creators.

References

Alexander, T. A. (2014). Linguistic pragmatism and cultural naturalism: Noncognitive experience, culture and the human eros. *European Journal of Pragmatism and American Philosophy, 2,* 64–90.

Biesta, G. (2006). Of all affairs, communication is the most wonderful: The communicative turn in dewey's democracy and education. In D. T. Hansen (Ed.), *John Dewey and our educational prospect: A critical engagement with Dewey's "democracy and education"* (pp. 23–28). Albany, NY: State University of New York Press.

Bleazby, J. (2011). Overcoming relativism and absolutism: Dewey's ideals of truth and meaning in philosophy for children. *Educational Philosophy and Theory, 43,* 453–466.

Cam, P. (1994). Dewey, Lipman, and the tradition of reflective education. In M. Taylor, H. Schrier, & P. Ghiraldelli Jr. (Eds.), *Pragmatism, education and children* (pp. 163–181). Amsterdam: Editions Rodopi B.V.

Cremin, L. A. (1964). *The transformation of the school: Progressivism in American education 1876–1957.* New York, NY: Vintage.

Dewey, J. (1988a). In J. A. Boydston (Ed.), *Experience and education, in John Dewey: The later works, vol. 13,* (pp. 1–62). Carbondale: Southern Illinois University Press.

Dewey, J. (1988b). Events and meanings. In J. A. Boydston (Ed.), *Essays on philosophy, education, and the orient 1921–1922, the middle works of John Dewey 1899-1924, vol. 13,* (pp. 276–280). Carbondale: Southern Illinois University Press.

Dewey, J. (1992). In L. Hickman (Ed.), *The correspondence of John Dewey, 1919–1939, volume II.* Carbondale: Southern Illinois University Press.

Dewey, J. (2008a). In J. A. Boydston (Ed.), *John Dewey: The middle works, 1899-1924, volume 9: 1899–1924: Democracy and education, 1916.* Carbondale: Southern Illinois University Press. (Original work published in 1916).

Dewey, J. (2008b). In J. A. Boydston (Ed.), *How we think, in John Dewey: The later works 1925–1953, volume 8: 1933* (pp. 105–352). Carbondale: Southern Illinois University Press..

Dreon, R. (2009). Dewey on language: Elements of a non-dualistic approach. *European Journal of Pragmatism and American Philosophy, 2,* 109–124.

Fitzsimons, P. (2000). Changing conceptions of globalization: Changing conceptions of education. *Educational Theory, 50,* 505–520.

Gaudelli, B., & Laverty, M. J. (2015). What is a global experience? *Education and Culture, 31,* 13–26.

Giddens, A. (1990). *The consequences of modernity.* Stanford, CA: Stanford University Press.

Greene, M. (1989). The teacher in John Dewey's works. *Teachers College Record, 90,* 24–35.

Gregory, M. (2000). The status of rational norms. *Analytic Teaching, 21,* 53–64.

Gregory, M., & Granger, D. (2012). Introduction: John Dewey on philosophy and childhood. *Education and Culture, 28*(2), 1–25.

Hansen, D. T. (2006). Introduction. In D. T. Hansen (Ed.), *John Dewey and our educational prospect: A critical engagement with Dewey's "democracy and education"* (pp. 1–22). Albany: State University of New York Press.

Hansen, D. T. (2009a). Education viewed through a cosmopolitan prism. In R. Glass (Ed.), *Philosophy of Education 2008* (pp. 206–214). Urbana, IL: Philosophy of Education Society.

Hansen, D. T. (2009b). Dewey and cosmopolitanism. *Education and Culture, 25,* 126–140.

Haynes, B. (2002). Globalisation and its consequences for scholarship in philosophy of education. *Educational Philosophy and Theory, 34,* 103–114..

Heath, G. (2002). Introduction to symposium on globalisation. *Educational Philosophy and Theory, 34,* 37–39.

Hickman, L. A. (2011). Scientific concepts in Dewey's pedagogy. In L. A. Hickman, M. C. Flamm, K. P. Skowroński, & J. A. Rea (Eds.), *The continuing relevance of John Dewey: Reflections on aesthetics, morality, science, and society* (pp. 193–204). Amsterdam, NY: Rodopi.

Hirst, P. H. (1967). The logical and psychological aspects of teaching a subject. In R. S. Peters (Ed.), *The concept of education* (pp. 44–60). New York, NY: Humanities Press.

Hytten, K. (2009). Deweyan democracy in a globalized world. *Educational Theory, 59*, 395–408.

Jackson, P. W. (2012). How we think we think. *Teachers College Record, 114*. Retrieved April 1, 2013, from http://www.tcrecord.org

Johnson, T. W. (1995). *Discipleship or pilgrimage? The educator's quest for philosophy*. Albany: State University of New York Press.

Johnson, M. (2009). Experiencing language: What's missing in linguistic pragmatism. *European Journal of Pragmatism and American Philosophy, 2*, 14–27.

Kilpatrick, W. H. (1918). The project method: The use of purposeful action in the educative process. *Teachers College Record, 18*, 319–335.

Laverty, M. J. (2014a). Philosophy in schools: Then and now. *Journal of Philosophy in Schools, 1*, 107–130.

Laverty, M. J. (2014b). Progressive education and its critics. In D. Phillips (Ed.), *Encyclopedia of educational theory and philosophy* (pp. 661–666). London: Sage.

Lipman, M. (1994). Philosophy for children's debt to Dewey. In M. Taylor, H. Schrier, & P. Ghiraldelli (Eds.), *Pragmatism, education and children* (pp. 143–151). Amsterdam: Editions Rodopi B.V.

Lipman, M., & Sharp, A. M. (1978). Some educational presuppositions of philosophy for children. *Oxford Review of Education, 4*, 85–90.

McDowell, J. (1996). *Mind and world*. Cambridge: Harvard University Press.

Nussbaum, M. (2010). *Not for profit: Why democracy needs the humanities*. Princeton, NJ: Princeton University Press.

O'Shea, J. R. (2014). A tension in pragmatist and neo-pragmatist conceptions of meaning and experience. *European Journal of Pragmatism and American Philosophy, 6*, 40–63.

Papastephanou, M. (2005). Globalization, globalism and cosmopolitanism as an educational ideal. *Educational Philosophy and Theory, 37*, 534–551.

Rizvi, F., & Lingard, B. (2000). Globalization and education: Complexities And Contingencies. *Educational Theory, 50*, 419–426.

Saito, N. (2006). Reawakening global awareness: Deweyan religious democracy reconsidered in the age of globalization. *Studies in Philosophy and Education, 25*, 129–144.

John Dewey and the Role of the Teacher in a Globalized World: Imagination, empathy, and 'third voice'

ANDREA R. ENGLISH

Abstract

Reforms surrounding the teacher's role in fostering students' social competences, especially those associated with empathy, have moved to the forefront of global higher education policy discourse. In this context, reform in higher education teaching has been focused on shifting teachers' practices away from traditional lecture-style teaching—historically associated with higher education teaching—towards student-centred pedagogical approaches, largely because of how the latter facilitate students' social learning, including the development of students' abilities connected to empathy, such as intercultural understanding. These developments towards learner-oriented higher education teaching may offer promising opportunities; however, a central problem within these current policy recommendations is that the connection between cultivating empathy and cultivating imagination is not explicitly foregrounded. Against this background, I turn to Dewey's notion of imagination to show how imagination is indispensable to all learning, and therefore has a role to play in teaching. In this article, I show how imagination is not only deeply connected to empathy, but also critical for gaining intercultural understanding and is a condition for the possibility that, as human beings, we can learn with and from others. On this basis, I argue that Dewey's notion of imagination provides significant insight on how to rethink what is needed to create inclusive classrooms in higher education, especially under conditions of cultural, linguistic and religious diversity. First, I consider Dewey's concept of learning and the indispensable role of imagination in learning. Second, drawing on the work of Martha Nussbaum, I examine how teaching through the narrative arts in higher education cultivates the imagination and helps us engage the lives of others. I use an example from my own teaching to illustrate how the narrative arts can foster dialogue across difference through the development of what I call 'third

Versions of this paper were presented as invited talks at the '2016 Centennial Conference on Democracy and Education' at the Annual Meeting of the *John Dewey Society* in Washington D.C., and at the 'Workshop on Democracy and Education' sponsored by the Universitaet Wien, Faculty of Philosophy and Educational Sciences and Niederoesteriechische Schule in der Schulentwicklung (NOESIS), in Vienna.

voice'—*a different or other 'position' that productively mediates reflective interaction between participants, including teacher and learners. In closing, I consider the implications of my discussion for present and future higher education policy on the evaluation of 'quality teaching'.*

Reforms surrounding the teacher's role in fostering students' social competences, especially those associated with empathy, have moved to the forefront of global higher education policy discourse (Hénard & Roseveare, 2012; Higher Level Group on the Modernisation of Higher Education [HLG], 2013). According to a report by the OECD,[1] these reforms are in part driven by the recent rapid increase in diverse populations of students coming together due to government support of student mobility—now a mainstay of global higher education internationalisation policy (American Council on Education [ACE], 2015; Hénard & Roseveare, 2012). In this context, reform in higher education teaching has been focused on shifting teachers' practices away from traditional lecture-style teaching—historically associated with higher education teaching—towards student-centred pedagogical approaches, largely because of how the latter facilitate students' social learning (Hénard & Roseveare, 2012, p. 9). In strong support of this shift to student-centred teaching, a 2013 report by the European Commission's 'Higher Level Group on the Modernisation of Higher Education', explicitly associates 'high-quality teaching' with the development of students' abilities connected to empathy, such as 'intercultural understanding' and 'understanding of different interests, views and ways of thinking' (HLG, 2013, p. 50).[2] These developments towards learner-oriented higher education teaching may offer promising opportunities—and, notably, they reference John Dewey's learning theory indicating his influence.[3] However, a central problem within these current policy recommendations is that the connection between cultivating *empathy* and cultivating *imagination* is not explicitly foregrounded. As a consequence, these recommendations could lead to policies that implicitly place an expectation on teachers which goes unrecognised or misinterpreted, namely the expectation to cultivate students' imagination. I contend that the teacher's task in cultivating the imagination needs to be made visible so that its role in guiding teachers' reflective practices can be critically evaluated by practitioners, theorists and policy-makers alike.

Against this background, I turn to Dewey's notion of imagination to show how imagination is indispensable to all learning, and therefore has a role to play in teaching. For Dewey, imagination can be seen as a 'pathway' to empathy—a connection underscored in a growing body of philosophical and psychological research on empathy.[4] In this paper, I show how imagination is not only deeply connected to empathy, but also critical for gaining intercultural understanding and is a condition for the possibility that, as human beings, we can learn with and from others. Therefore, Dewey's notion of imagination provides significant insight on how to rethink what is needed to create inclusive classrooms in higher education, especially under conditions of cultural, linguistic and religious diversity.

In section one, I provide an in-depth examination of Dewey's notion of the connections between learning, imagination and empathy. I focus on illuminating how imagination helps us reflectively engage moments of resistance in our experiences, especially by aiding our empathetic exploration of what I call 'the in-between realm of learning', in which the ideas and views of others emerge. In section two, I turn to consider the teacher's role in cultivating students' imagination and how this connects to fostering dialogue across difference. Drawing primarily on the work of Martha Nussbaum, I examine how teaching through the narrative arts in higher education cultivates the imagination and helps us engage the lives of others. I develop the idea that when teaching productively cultivates imagination, it creates what I refer to as *third voice*, a different or other 'position' that productively mediates interaction between participants, including teacher and learners. I provide an example from my own teaching experiences to help illustrate how *third voice* serves to facilitate critical reflection within cross-cultural learning contexts. I close the section by pointing out central challenges teachers in higher education face when seeking to facilitate dialogue across difference. In the third and final section, I consider the implications of my discussion for present and future higher education policy on the evaluation of 'quality teaching'.

Exploring within the In-between of Learning: The Role of Imagination in Thinking and Learning

Dewey's theory of learning provides unique insight into the complex connection between learning, imagination and empathy. Underlying this connection, as I seek to draw out here, is the idea that human experience involves arriving at the limits to our knowledge and ability—it involves an encounter with our own 'blind spots'.[5] This experience of limitation is constitutive of learning, and imagination is a central human capacity, which helps us navigate this experience and address our 'blind spots' in a way that incorporates others. In order to get at these complex links between learning, imagination and empathy more fully, I address each of these notions in turn, proceeding in three main steps. First, I attend to Dewey's concept of learning as a process he calls a 'reflective experience'. I then turn to examine how Dewey defines imagination, highlighting how it plays a role in fostering reflective exploration within what I refer to as the 'in-between realms of learning'. Finally, I develop the connections between imagination and empathy, by focusing on how imagination, in Dewey's view, is a capacity, which allows us to grasp the world from the situation of others. On this basis, I argue that imagination is central to learning from and with others. This argument in turn provides the foundation for my view that teaching involves the cultivation of the imagination, which I will turn to in part two.

Learning, Thinking and the In-between

In *Democracy and Education*, Dewey gives an account of the connection between learning and experience that clarifies how all learning involves encounters with difference and otherness, in which we experience moments of resistance that, in turn, open us up to questioning our taken-for-granted ideas and habitual ways of being. He explains that experience is both active and passive: active, in that it involves an interaction between self and world in which we 'try' something in the world, and passive, in that we 'undergo' something from the world in return (e.g. Dewey, 1916/2008, pp. 146, 147). Moments of doing and undergoing occur in a range of everyday interactions with the world, from the more mundane—for example, when we grab an object that we thought was smooth, yet it turns out to be rough—to the more significant—for example, when we trusted a friend with a secret and find out it has been shared with others.

Dewey repeatedly uses the example of a child sticking his finger into a flame in order to demonstrate the connection between doing and undergoing, which is central to his concept of learning. The undergoing side of experience is the feeling of a pain of a burn, that resulted from an act of 'doing' something, namely putting one's finger into the fire (Dewey, 1916/2008, p. 146). Without connecting the pain of the burn to the act of touching the flame, the child does not learn; however, if the child reflects and considers why his finger was in pain after touching the flame, then the child is beginning a process of learning *from* the interaction with the world. For Dewey, these basic elements are in all learning processes, whether of an adult or child.

While Dewey's concept of learning is commonly connected to the idea of 'doing' and 'active learning' (and is even referred to as 'learning by doing'), the experience of 'undergoing' is particularly significant for understanding learning in its connection to imagination (which I discuss below). When we 'undergo', this means we have come across something we could not foresee; it 'tells' us that we do not have control, we are not able to correctly anticipate, we do not have accurate foresight and we are not able to calculate how our interaction with the world will unfold. Resistance tells us that routine and habit are not sufficient to engage the world because the world is not how we thought it was. These moments in which the world defies our expectations and we encounter a 'blind spot' mark a beginning of learning. Dewey describes this beginning of learning as an encounter with something unexpected which brings us into a state of 'doubt', 'uncertainty' or 'confusion' in which we ask ourselves: What happened? What went wrong? (Dewey, 1916/2008, pp. 155–157; English, 2013). These encounters with the unexpected point to the fact that learning begins as a discontinuous moment in experience; this discontinuity arises when we encounter something new and unfamiliar —a new object, idea, concept or behaviour of another person (English, 2013).

But it is important to note that these beginnings to learning, which arise from our encounter with difference and otherness, are just that, namely *beginnings*; they do not constitute what Dewey calls a reflective learning experience. Yet, still, as beginnings to learning, these moments of discontinuity or interruption have educative value: such moments offer us the opportunity to take in something new—the new idea or object that initially confuses us—in a way that can transform our thinking and modes of acting. The central question then is: How do we treat experiences of discontinuity and resistance so that they inform our thinking?

In order for these moments of discontinuity to develop into learning processes, we need to make a reflective connection between what we did in the world and how the world responded to us in return. To make a connection between doing and undergoing, we must first explore *possible* connections through a type of thinking that Dewey calls 'reflection'. 'Reflection', or 'reflective thinking', for Dewey, is the form of thinking that takes up the doubt and uncertainty arising from our experience of limitation. Reflective activity is situated in the moment in which we became uncertain and it actively engages the particularities of that moment, rather than ignoring them or moving on by trial and error. To 'reflect' is to attempt to enquire into the uncertainty and explore it with the purpose of determining what it is that caused us to become uncertain or perplexed: 'the perplexities of the situation suggest certain ways out. We try these ways, and either push our way out, in which case we know we have found what we were looking for, or the situation gets darker and more confused—in which case we know we are still ignorant' (Dewey, 1916/2008, pp. 155, 156). When our thinking processes are so engaged as to try to understand the situation we are in such that we remain in 'suspense' and investigate our own blind spots, then thinking becomes a 'reflective experience' (Dewey, 1916/2008, pp. 152–155). Reflection seeks to illuminate how the self and world relate, that is, it seeks to articulate how the 'change made [to the world] by [our] action' relates to 'a change made in us' (Dewey, 1916/2008, p. 147). By 'reflecting', that is, by making this 'backward and forward connection' between what we did and what we underwent in consequence, new meaning arises (Dewey, 1916/2008, pp. 146, 147). A reflective experience is the term Dewey uses to describe genuine learning processes which entail the back and forth of doing and undergoing and making connections.

While Dewey scholarship has largely recognised that Dewey, like other pragmatists, views thinking as beginning in our moments of doubt and uncertainty, less considered is the educative significance of this moment as an opening, as a space of ambiguity—a space of being *between* old and new ideas and beliefs. Dewey refers to this space using the idea of the 'twilight zone of inquiry' (Dewey, 1916/2008, p. 155; English, 2013, 2016b). Reflective learning experiences are educative because, in them, we reflectively explore this space in order to understand the nature of our interaction with the world. I describe this realm of uncertainty as an *in-between* realm of learning; it is a space in which we are between old and new, right and wrong, in which we have recognised that old values and beliefs no longer guide us, but have not yet found new ways forward (English, 2013, 2016b). In this space, we can ask new questions that can lead us to discover previously unforeseen connections and associations between things, which can guide how we come to think and act. This process of enquiry, exploration and discovery requires imagination in order to be fruitful, as I discuss further below.

Before turning to examine Dewey's concept of imagination and how it connects to this 'in-between realm of learning', it is worth emphasising a point that will prove particularly relevant to the discussion of imagination: Dewey's concept of learning and its connection to experience highlight the fact that undergoing the world has moral significance—it points us to our 'blind spots' and we must consider these if we want to learn from the world and others. As mentioned, the *undergoing* aspect of human experience describes the moments in which the world in some way defies our expectations; it resists us in some way. Dewey also refers to these moments as 'suffering', a term that more strongly indicates that when the world surprises us, we are affected. Undergoing, or suffering, for Dewey, points to the moments when we 'take in' the world as other. In *Art as Experience*, Dewey describes the connection between 'taking in' and undergoing the world as follows:

> There is [...] an element of undergoing, of suffering in its large sense, in every experience. Otherwise there would be no taking in of what preceded. For 'taking in' in any vital experience is something more than placing something on the top of consciousness over what was previously known. It involves reconstruction which may be painful. (Dewey, 1934/2008, pp. 47, 48)

'Taking in' means taking in difference and newness in a way that is transformative. Taking in arises from undergoing the world in a genuine sense such that it affects us and changes how we think and act, and as Dewey says, this can be 'painful'. The alternative to 'taking in' the world as different and other is ignoring or escaping the felt resistance, and thus not learning: we either have a 'zeal for *doing*', in which case, we treat resistance 'as an obstruction to be beaten down, not as an invitation to reflection', or, we *undergo* to such an extreme that we are led to escape the felt resistance of the world by escaping into 'day dreaming' without the new 'taking root in mind' (Dewey, 1934/2008, p. 51).

Given this, Dewey's concepts of learning as a reflective experience can be viewed as a deep theoretical consideration of how human beings can reflectively take up potentially painful experiences of limitation, which disrupt our habitual and taken-for-granted ways of thinking and being and call upon us to learn. Do we run from resistance and ignore possibilities to learn from otherness or difference, or do we remain in suspense and explore new ways of thinking, acting and being? How we answer this question becomes even more significant in cross-cultural contexts, when we potentially have the opportunity to learn from others' cultures, values, experiences and beliefs that may be different from our own. Imagination plays a critical role in aiding our ability to learn from and with others, as I explore in detail next.

Imagination and the In-between

Imagination, on Dewey's account, connects specifically to the undergoing side of experience, in which we experience resistance; it helps us take in the world in a way that is called for by 'undergoing'.[6] Our capacity for imagination allows us to dwell in the space of the in-between because it facilitates our ability to extend our thinking beyond the known, and allows alternative ways of seeing and being in the world to emerge in our minds. As I will draw out below, imagination fosters reflective learning experiences; it enriches our thinking and thereby enriches our capacity to explore and understand the perplexity and uncertainty we have encountered within experience.

In his definition of imagination, Dewey draws our attention to this idea of imagination as extending experience by 'taking in' the world: 'Imagination' is not 'the imaginary', rather it is 'a warm and intimate taking in of the *full scope* of a situation' (Dewey, 1916/2008, p. 244, emphasis mine). Two contrasts, one explicit and one implicit, come to the fore in Dewey's definition of imagination that point to the connections between imagination and learning: the explicit contrast between imagination and the imaginary and the implicit contrast between a full scope of a situation and a narrow scope. I turn to the latter point first, and then discuss the distinction between imagination and the imaginary, which will lead into my discussion in part two on the role of teaching through the arts to cultivate imagination.

In Dewey's definition of imagination above, the idea of the 'full scope of a situation' is contrasted with a more narrow scope that we gain in our everyday personal experiences. By pulling us towards the full scope of a situation, imagination always brings us beyond what Dewey calls 'the scope of personal, vitally direct experience' which is 'very limited' (Dewey, 1916/2008, p. 240). Dewey's notion of imagination as an extension of the direct, personal 'here and now' helps us understand imagination as the capacity which allows us to extend our thinking processes into the in-between realm of experience, wherein we are still lost, still uncertain, still searching for ways of understanding our experience of difference. Imagination thus seeks to move us beyond the narrow, limited and the habitual, which arise from repetitive existence. 'Narrowed' experiences, in the Deweyan sense, are experiences that have become 'acclimat[ed] to standardised meaning' (Fesmire, 2003, p. 66). Being wedded to standardised meanings in the world limits our capacity for growth and learning. This frames our thinking so that we merely see the old in the new, rather than allowing the new to be *new*, that is, to be unfamiliar, unknown, different and strange—to be the object of learning.[7] If we go on living within the confines of narrow, direct personal experience, then we never encounter our own 'blind spots'. Without such experiences of limitation, we do not come to question what we have taken for granted, and therefore cannot learn from other human beings (English, 2013). Through imagination, the 'old and familiar things' that we have taken for granted 'are made new in experience' (Dewey, 1916/2008, p. 271). In this way, as Maxine Greene underscores, 'imagination more than any other capacity breaks through the "inertia of habit"' (Greene, 1995, p. 21).

Let us now take a look at the explicit distinction Dewey makes in his definition of imagination above, the distinction between imagination and the imaginary. Dewey's contrast between 'imagination' and the 'imaginary' points to an important connection between imagination and the experience of resistance, that as I discussed, is part of learning. Imagination is not simply the 'imaginary', that is, it is not being in a state of pure fancy or daydreaming in a way that has no connection to the situation at hand— what we see, hear, think, remember and feel. Unlike imagination, the imaginary strays too far from our lived experiences and so it does not deal with the material in the world that resists us and defies our expectations, that is, the material of learning and growth: the 'mind stays aloof' toying with material that 'does not offer enough resistance, and so mind plays with it capriciously' (Dewey, 1916/2008, p. 272). Imagination, in contrast, takes up the stuff of experience, directly connecting the moments of resistance that are part of human experience.

Unlike the realm of the imaginary, which is an escape from experience, the realm of imagination opens up as an explicit 'taking in' of the world we have undergone, a world that is new, that is different from what we had experienced before, such that we experience discontinuity and resistance. Imagination, as 'taking in of the full scope of a situation', *means* integrating those moments of the unexpected (which disrupt or interrupt the smooth path of habitual modes of thinking and action) into processes of learning, in turn giving them more meaning. In this way, imagination promotes what Dewey refers to as 'integral experience'. An integral experience is neither aimless nor arbitrarily restrictive as if forcing us to rigidly remain within certain predefined limits; rather, it is an experience of growth towards 'maturation', or what Dewey calls, a 'consummation' (Dewey, 1934/2008, pp. 47–49). For Dewey, this experience is 'aesthetic' in that it does not ignore resistance, but rather it attends to it, and converts 'resistance and tensions [...] into a movement toward an inclusive and fulfilling close' (Dewey, 1934/2008, p. 62). Imagination is essential to aesthetic experiences; it extends our capacity to take in the resistance, tension, conflict and struggle that is initiated by our encounters with those things that are new and different, that are difficult to understand, that contradict our beliefs, cause uncertainty, incite fear or shut us down emotionally in ways that prevent our ability to learn.

Imagination and Empathy

Dewey's concept of imagination illuminates the idea that the work of imagination as 'taking in' is an act of empathetically learning from others. It involves taking in the perspectives, feelings and interests of others. As Dewey writes, we do not come to understand another person, even one 'with which we habitually associate', just by having more information about him or her (Dewey, 1934/2008, p. 339). We come to understand another person and gain 'friendship and intimate affection' when, by way of imagination, our knowledge of the person is integrated into our empathetic viewpoint:

> It is when the desires and aims, the interests and modes of response of another become an expansion of our own being that we understand him. We learn to see with his eyes, hear with his ears, and their results give true instruction, for they are built into our own structure (Dewey, 1934/2008, p. 339).

It is this idea that captures what Fesmire calls 'empathetic projection' or empathy, as one of the two central meanings of imagination in Dewey's work (Fesmire, 2003, p. 65).[8] Empathetic projection is not an act of applying one's own values onto others, but rather of 'taking the attitudes of others', which 'stirs us beyond numbness so we pause to sort through others' aspirations, interests, and worries as our own' (Fesmire, 2003, p. 65). In this connection between imagination and the gaining of affection towards others, we can see why Dewey uses the terms 'warm and intimate' in describing the sort of 'taking in' of the world that imagination entails—imagination brings us together as human beings. In what follows, this is what I will refer to as empathy, even though Dewey, in his time, referred to it as sympathy.[9] I define empathy as the imaginative seeing of situations from the view of another person, or, as Dewey phrases it, 'imaginatively' putting ourselves 'in the situations of others' (Dewey & Tufts, 1908/2008, p. 150).

In examining Dewey's notion of imagination as an essential part of the process of learning as reflective experience, the relation between imagination and reflective thinking becomes apparent: they stand in a dialectic relation to each other. As mentioned above, reflective thinking, for Dewey, is a form of thinking that directly addresses the resistance, perplexity and discontinuity in our experiences and connects it to our activity in the world. Imagination, in its act of in taking in the full scope of a situation, inclusive of the ideas and feelings of others, provides us with various ways of understanding the felt resistance of the world, and thus offers us more multifarious and deeper meanings as to what our blind spots may consist in. In offering us this insight into our own blind spots, it extends our understanding of the bearing of these on our future choices, thus feeding our reflective activity. In turn, reflection takes the increased meaning implied in the situation at hand to make more associations between what we did and what we have undergone, thus feeding imagination's further contemplation of 'what ifs'.[10] Together, imagination and reflection foster learning within the in-between realm. They extend this realm so that within it, we can consider possibilities for understanding ourselves and our relation to the world. Imagination and reflection acting in this dialectic interchange preclude us from simply moving on via a reiteration of our habitual modes of thinking and acting. By calling upon us to consider our blind spots, they engender the sort of change and reconstructive transformation that, for Dewey, is part of the idea of education itself: education 'is that reconstruction or reorganisation of experience which adds to the meaning of experience, and which increases ability to direct the course of subsequent experience' (Dewey, 1916/2008, p. 82).

Dewey's definition of imagination as the extension of experience beyond our limited and habitual world of everyday life makes vivid the fact that without imagination, human beings cannot move past the realm of the known and familiar, that is, they cannot learn from others. Imagination extends our thinking so that we can consider and *take in* that which is *beyond* what is immediately within our mind's grasp, reshaping what we take for granted as true and known, through the lens of other possible experiences informed by the situation of others. In this way, imagination is, as Thomas Alexander writes, 'temporally complex', integrating past, present and anticipated future, so that 'activity may unfold in the most meaningful and value-rich way possible' (Alexander, 1993, p. 386). Imagination brings us from known and visible, towards the unknown, invisible and uncertain that lies beyond our immediate ways of thinking and being, helping us dwell in these spaces of uncertainty as spaces of learning.

Considering all of the above-mentioned connections between imagination and learning, we must also note, finally, that, for Dewey, there is no arrival at the full scope of a situation; imagination helps us seek the full scope of a situation, but it does not ensure we will attain it. Even as we attempt to take in the full scope of experience, we are also always necessarily continuing to grow. As beings that are capable of learning, that is perfectible, or 'plastic', as Dewey calls it, human beings never arrive at an end point to knowledge and understanding; there are always things that we could still come to know and learn, and thus there is always a chance that there is yet a *fuller* scope of the situation than what we presently perceive.[11] Because we cannot ever know if we are actually taking in the full scope of a situation, our imagination is markedly critical. It is by way of imagination that we try to determine what we may have left out of our present picture of how things are. Imagination helps us ask creative questions to consider wherein our blind spots may lie. To do this well, however, we need to *cultivate* our imagination. As Alexander notes, for imagination 'to interpret a situation in terms of possibilities in turn requires an organised body of experience upon which to draw. The richer this background is, 'the more nuances and complex our perception of the world is' (Alexander, 1993, p. 386). Therefore, for rich imagination, we need rich experiences, which must be built up in educative learning environments. Given this, the question of how we cultivate imagination—by which methods and in which directions—becomes of vital significance for educators. This is especially true in today's learning environments, wherein there are potentially greater gaps between the cultural experiences of teachers and students, which, without the cultivation of imagination, could hinder participants' abilities to learn with and from one another.[12] Next, I examine possibilities for cultivating the imagination in higher education teaching contexts.

Imagination as 'Empathetic Projection' and the Creation of 'Third Voice': Teaching through the Arts to Support Learning across Cultures in Higher Education

As I have argued, imagination is essential for going outside one's present knowledge and ability to suspend judgement and consider alternative ways of thinking. As Dewey helps us see, imagination connects to empathy; it is a form of 'empathetic projection', giving us 'access' to a view of the world as others may see it. With this connection to empathy, imagination facilitates transformative learning processes that happen through our interactions with others, and thereby it makes possible our ability to learn with and from others. In this section, I turn to explore the role of the narrative arts in cultivating imagination as empathetic projection. I briefly consider Dewey's view of the special place of the arts in enriching our view of the world and our interactions with others. I then draw upon the more recent work of Martha Nussbaum, who, in her well-known theory of human capabilities, places imagination at the centre of the human capacity to understand the experience of others.[13] With Nussbaum, I consider the special role of the narrative arts in cultivating our imagination. I argue that the narrative arts help cultivate what I call *third voice*, an important feature of environments that have opportunities for rich cross-cultural experiences of learning. To illustrate the meaning of this concept and how it gets realised in practice, I provide an example from my own practice of teaching through the arts in higher education. To close the section, I address central challenges for teaching in higher education classrooms today.

Many thinkers have long considered the arts as significant in cultivating imagination in a way that supports the development of our capacity for empathy. Dewey was no exception, and while he considered all subject areas as having an educative capacity to build our imagination, he granted a special place to the arts. The arts extend our experiences by supplying us with 'organs of vision' (Dewey, 1916/2008, p. 247). Through engagement with the arts, we gain new insight and enrich our ways of understanding the world and others around us. The arts have a particular way of helping us experience difference, especially anything that differs from our ordinary everyday world. The arts allow us to 'enter, through imagination and the emotions they evoke, into other forms of relationships and participation than our own' (Dewey, 1934/2008, p. 336). In this way, the arts support 'appreciation' as an 'enhancement of the qualities which make an ordinary experience [...] capable of *full* assimilation' through the medium of imagination (Dewey, 1916/2008, p. 246, emphasis mine; also, see also, pp. 244, 245). Dewey's remarks illuminate the idea that the arts provide us with various 'lenses' for *taking in* the world of experience, and this means seeing things we had not previously seen; they reveal 'a depth and range of meaning in experiences which otherwise might be mediocre and trivial' (Dewey, 1934/2008, p. 245)

In her work on the arts and imagination, Nussbaum contributes to a way of understanding and educating the human capacity to learn from the other. Similar to Dewey, but without reference to his work, Nussbaum argues that the arts cultivate our imagination by opening our minds to alternative ways of thinking and to possibilities that we had not previously foreseen. Nussbaum focuses on the narrative arts, describing them as having particular force in opening the mind through imagination. Engagement with stories of others' lives, she argues, allows the reader to become aware of the fact that there are others that think, act and are subject to different circumstances than the reader may be (Nussbaum, 1997, p. 88).

Nussbaum's argument underscores the idea that our engagement with stories facilitates our gaining of an empathetic view, but it is not gained merely by way of the acquisition of more information about others, but rather by encountering our own blind spots. Central to Nussbaum's theory of the role of the narrative arts in human development is the fact that something previously 'hidden from view' is revealed to the reader—that is, the reader becomes aware of that which was in his or her blind spot. Through engagement with the arts, our imagination is sparked and we become aware of the things beyond our immediate perception and beyond what our everyday experience provides. Nussbaum points out that the narrative arts, especially those works that 'unsettle' and 'disturb' our sensibilities, have the ability to reveal to us characters with a 'rich inner life', one to which we may not typically have access (Nussbaum, 1997, p. 100). Literary scenarios can reveal the inner lives of others as complex, and associated with emotions of 'hope and fear, happiness and distress', as well as 'traits such as courage, self-restraint, dignity, perseverance and fairness' (Nussbaum, 1997, p. 90). Learning about the inner lives of others cultivates a sense of wonder and imagination with which we can connect the lives of others in stories to our own everyday 'attempts to explain the world and [our] own actions in it' (Nussbaum, 1997, p. 89).[14]

Nussbaum's discussion of engaging with the narrative arts describes a certain kind of confrontation with difference that is connected to the Deweyan notion of reflective learning processes discussed above. This type of interaction with difference helps us think beyond what we know and helps us imaginatively consider new possibilities. Such interactions initially *interrupt* us and call upon us to become other to ourselves by questioning our taken-for-granted beliefs (English, 2013). Thus, creating space for imagining the world as different than how we may immediately perceive it in everyday life has educative value: it facilitates our understanding of the fact that things *can* be hidden from view—that is, that we can have blind spots and are fallible. The recognition of our fallibility can be painful. It makes us vulnerable and unsettled. Yet, I argue that this recognition is a pre-condition for the development of empathy. Empathy requires the capacity to see things from another person's perspective, while maintaining difference between self and other,[15] and this means genuinely considering the possibility that 'I could be wrong'. When one considers that there can be other views of the world that could enhance one's own view, or even counter it in a way that is productive, one creates openings for 'taking in', that is, learning from the other.

JOHN DEWEY'S DEMOCRACY AND EDUCATION IN AN ERA OF GLOBALIZATION

Creating 'Third Voice' to Support Cross-Cultural Understanding

Nussbaum's idea of texts as having the capacity to reveal to us what is 'hidden from view' hints at what I am calling the creation of *third voice*. The *third voice* is the voice offered through the text that is in some way 'other' than the voices represented in any particular group. Third voice is educative in that it offers us insight into what may reside within our blind spots, that is, the things we do not know, cannot see and have difficulty imagining on our own without the aide of the text. In what follows, I give an example from my own teaching showing how this *third voice* was created and how it facilitated intercultural dialogue and learning. The teaching and learning that I detail below was not part of any formal self-study, or action research or intended to be research of any kind; rather, it is my best attempt at reflecting on my time in a class with students, that, looking back, I would now describe as one in which all participants (the students and I, as the teacher) increasingly developed empathy for one another through the imaginative experience of *third voice*.

In my several years of experience teaching in higher education, prior to the classroom situation I describe here, I had been actively developing a pedagogical approach to teaching philosophy of education through the arts using drama, film, music, visual arts, literature and more. As my classrooms became more diverse with regard to the linguistic, religious and cultural backgrounds of the students, I began to experiment more with approaching aspects of the subject matter using the narrative arts, especially autobiographies. In one of my courses in particular, I saw how this created openings for thinking, imagination as empathetic projection and reciprocity that took place *between* the students, and between the students and me, that I had not experienced without this approach. The course focused on the concept of 'critical thinking', and we read from the tradition of Critical Theory, including works by Theodor Adorno and Hannah Arendt. In order for students to understand the history and the lives behind these thinkers' ideas, I assigned the autobiography of Walter Benjamin, which is written as a series of episodes from his memories of childhood in early twentieth Century Berlin, to be read alongside the often dense philosophical ideas presented in the other texts.[16]

In the beginning of the course, students seemed divided, as is often the case at the beginning, but when students of diverse backgrounds are present, the division, in my experience, tends to come along lines of speaking. Those from the dominant culture and country spoke freely, and appeared comfortable questioning my views and the subject matter, and those from other backgrounds were mostly silently listening.[17] In this class, as in many others I had had, there was a mix of male and female international students, who self-identified[18] as Muslim, and who were not native speakers of the national language, as well as male and female 'home' students, who spoke the national language as a mother tongue, some of whom indicated having secular or Christian upbringing. I do not identify with a particular religion, was not raised within a particular religious context and I was not a native of the country in which I was teaching. In mentioning this, my intent is not to reduce the students, or myself, to these categories, but rather my intent is to provide background to a situation that offers different kinds of challenges to teachers than those faced within culturally and religiously homogeneous classroom contexts. These challenges include, among other things, knowing how to ensure that all students are included and able to feel a sense of being an equal participant in the classroom environment. In this class, just as in others with similar conditions of diversity, I noticed the atmosphere was one of students appearing distant and unfamiliar with one another. I learned from experience that, left unattended, unwanted power structures could develop implicitly and hinder educative dialogue and learning between students.

Each week as we read Benjamin's autobiography, I provided students with the option of choosing how they would share their thoughts about his world, using an activity called 'Reading Circles', which allows students to take on different reading roles to engage a text. For one of these roles, students had the option of providing a non-linguistic, artistic response to the text, which they would bring to class and show to others as a basis for full class discussion. One student created an artwork accompanied by music to illuminate Benjamin's image of childhood. Another brought photographs of her return to her birth country to discuss the idea of 'home' and the experience of being an outsider in a new place. Another student brought an apple pie that she had baked to represent a difficult experience from childhood that she recalled when reading Benjamin's story, and yet another designed an elaborate labyrinth image detailing the complexity of being lost, which was an interpretation of the thread running through Benjamin's life story.

As the weeks proceeded, unexpectedly, students not only began to imagine and understand the historical context of the lives of Benjamin and the other authors we were reading, but by discussing the similarities and differences between *their worlds* and *his*, they also began to identify ways they were similar and different from one another, ways that cut across cultural norms. Over time, they became closer with and more trusting of one another and me.[19] I explain the reason for this now, looking back, as a result of an 'expanded space' that was created by the cultivation of the imagination as an *empathetic projection* into the world of others. In understanding how they shared, and did not share, experiences with a third—an other, Walter Benjamin —who was neither 'me' nor 'you', and who was not physically part of our classroom, the students began to reconfigure and expand our space together, to a space which included all of us, Benjamin, the other authors and those in the world who were represented by them, especially those who experienced injustice.[20] Our classroom became a place where students began to reflect upon and critique their own experiences and upbringing, and each of them identified failings in how they were educated, including problematic standards of historical truth, ideas of human rights and justice and restrictions on freedom of enquiry.

Through this example, I seek to highlight how literature, especially the literary form of autobiography, has the capacity to create *third voice*, a voice that is otherwise not present in the classroom. Third voice has the function of inspiring other 'voices', those views and ideas that are beyond the realm of our direct experiences, and may not have come about without initiation from the third voice. These other voices were represented in students' responses to the text, artistic responses that allowed for increased openings in the minds of the others in the room (myself and the other students). Third voice does not need to be created through story, though I see story as particularly productive. Rather, it can be created through any material that pulls participants towards the creation of a shared horizon of meanings and facilitates understandings of what it means to be human. In this way, third voice inspires empathy as 'the desirable quality [that] is more than mere feeling; it is cultivated imagination for what [people] have in common and a rebellion at whatever divides them' (Dewey, 1916/2008, pp. 127, 128; see also Dewey 1934/2008, p. 275).

Third voice enhances relationships and participation by initiating a move from thinking to thinking together. In creating new openings for new perspectives, the third voice leads to communicatively thinking together and exploring our blind spots as a group, which in turn leads to the discovery of additional pathways for thinking. It allows us to imaginatively extend our experiences of the present world into a world that is 'hidden from view'. As members of the group respond to this extension and creatively address the resistance felt within it, they offer others a way to extend their experiences. When teachers create 'third voice', they foster imagination, which Greene sees as vital to use 'in a search for openings without which our lives narrow and our pathways become cul-de-sacs' (Greene, 1995, p. 17). The third voice mediates relationships between the teacher and learner and between learners such that all, in different ways, learn with and from each other.

In this class, I aimed for the students to understand critical thinking. What actually happened was that not only did they understand it, they began to enact it. A traditional thinker might ask: What does 'apple pie' have to do with higher education? In this case, it allowed one student to connect to a world she previously knew little about, and in doing so, she was able to creatively reinterpret the earlier oppressive experience of her youth. By providing students with opportunities to see other possible ways of viewing themselves and others through extended 'organs of vision', they become critical in productive ways. Dewey describes,

> a sense of possibilities that are unrealized and that might be realized are when they are put in contrast with actual conditions, the most penetrating 'criticism' of the latter that can be made. It is by a sense of possibilities *opening* before us that we become aware of constrictions that hem us in and of burdens that oppress. (Dewey, 1934/2008, p. 349, emphasis mine)

Upon reflection, this opening is what I recognised in my students.

One of the central challenges teachers face when creating classrooms that allow students to engage across linguistic, cultural and religious diversity is to help students make the move from 'thinking' to 'thinking together'. Dialogue and engagement with the arts are central to supporting this move. In my own courses, through communicating about students' linguistic and artistic contributions inspired by autobiographies, or also by artworks, films, photographs and other forms of art, students support the critical growth of shared meanings and understandings—including understandings of feelings, ideas, hopes and fears—that are cultivated by imagination.[21] But these shared meanings are not a result of conformity to the majority nor can finding it be forced by a teacher. Rather, they result from sharing in 'the arts of living', sharing in 'communication and participation in the values of life by means of the imagination' (Dewey, 1934/2008, p. 339; see also Dewey, 1925/2008, p. 132). Such communication and participation is the condition for the possibility to learn in groups with others in any discipline. What is learned in educative peer interaction, aside from any particular disciplinary knowledge, is how to have an experience with integrity, an experience in which self and others—one's own and others ideas, questions, feelings, interests, experiences, concerns and shifts in perspective—are treated as valuable.

To accomplish all this also requires, what Deborah Britzman calls, 'pedagogic imagination', with which educators imagine the relations between what *is* and what *is possible* within interactions with students (Britzman, 1991, p. 87; see also Griffiths, 2014). Imagination allows us to reflectively explore within the 'in-between realm of learning', wherein the problem may not be determined, the paths and possibilities not fully recognised, where we have *undergone* something, but do not yet fully understand our experience and have not yet devised a way out. This affective, moral and cognitive space is not a space seeking immediate resolution but seeking further openings in the mind.[22] Imagination is educative because it functions not only to help us conceive of concrete possibilities, but also to conceive of *the possibility of possibility*, that is, that there could be more still out of my view, still within my blind spot.

Conclusion: Implications for Higher Education Policy

As member states in the European Union press forward to professionalise higher education teachers by 2020, and at the same time create plans for evaluation of quality teaching practice, it is critical that teachers understand the full expectations embedded within these policies. From my discussion, it should be clear that I believe a conscious move in higher education policy towards dialogic classrooms (which support group learning) and away from transmissive forms of teaching—(whether in lecture format or not) in general is positive. Such policies have the potential to support teachers in building cooperative and inclusive classrooms, which foster listening and sensitivity towards others. But there are other trends in global educational policy that may be compromising these goals, namely: the trend towards international comparative data in higher education. The sorts of policies that have adversely affected primary and secondary schools, which place schools in public competition with one another, and make teachers' jobs dependent upon test outcomes are soon going to be taken up in higher education, albeit with a slightly different face. The United Kingdom, for example, has developed the 'Teaching Excellence Framework [TEF]' as part of its reform agenda (DBIS, 2016). Although the TEF is still in planning and piloting phases, it appears to be set to publicise ratings of the evaluation of teaching quality within UK universities, in an effort to facilitate competition between universities for student enrolment. The problem with this is not the evaluation of teaching per se, which is necessary and valuable for teachers' growth and professionalisation. Rather, the problem that I suspect will arise is the same one that has arisen in primary and secondary schools in many parts of the world, including in the UK: the problem is that the criteria according to which external evaluators evaluate teaching quality will be those that are associated with transmissive, direct lecture-style teaching—which furnishes clear, organised, pre-packed easily digestible bits of knowledge measurable in standardised ways—and not those that are associated with dialogic, active teaching and learning.

The latter is much harder to assess; when it is successful, it includes the less visible, moral and ethical dimensions of teaching that are engaged when teachers cultivate imagination, experimental and critical thinking and the building of empathetic relationships across difference.

Dewey scholar, Robert Boostrom, recently wrote, 'our world, our culture, our selves depend on playful, fanciful, arbitrary, dangerous imagination' (Boostrom, 2014, p. 92). Imagination is dangerous to those who do not wish to see diverse groups come together, think together, communicate and cooperate in democratic, educative ways. It was not just in Dewey's time, but also one hundred years later in our own, that our world becomes 'uncivil because human beings are divided into non-communicating sects, races, nations, classes and cliques' (Dewey, 1934/2008, p. 339). Understanding imagination, as I have suggested here, can help us understand how, as a group, teachers and learners become uncertain and imagine possibilities, an experience that is in itself educative.[23]

Disclosure statement

No potential conflict of interest was reported by the author.

Notes

1. OECD stands for 'The Organisation for Economic Co-operation and Development' and consists of the work of 34 member countries and 70 non-member economies, see http://usoecd.usmission.gov/mission/overview.html.
2. See also pages pp. 32 and 35. The report draws on terminology from the seven competences of lifelong learners in the European Key Competence Framework. The terminology surrounding ideas of empathy appear to be drawn from one of the key competences, 'Social and Civic Competence', which describes 'the core skills of this competence include the ability to communicate constructively in different environments, to show tolerance, express and understand different viewpoints, to negotiate with the ability to create confidence and to feel empathy' (EPEC, 2006). See also the Higher Education Academy's Internationalising Higher Education Framework, which promotes activities of intercultural engagement 'underpinned by empathy, sociability and sensitivity to all forms of diversity' in all contexts of higher education institutions. (HEA, 2014).
3. See the epigraphs in HLG (2013).
4. See, e.g. Smith (2011) and Prinz (2011). See also earlier work in philosophy of education, e.g. Gallo (1994) and Greene (1995).
5. I have referred to the experience of limitation elsewhere using the idea of the negativity of one's experience, which connects to a long-standing tradition of philosophy of education (English, 2013). Here, I use the terminology of blind spots metaphorically because it is particularly useful to capture both the individual aspect of experience—my blind spot is particular to my own learning history—and the interconnection between oneself and the world—I only recognise that I had a blind spot on the basis of an encounter with a world and others that are in some way unfamiliar to me, and thus present me with a limit to my knowledge and experience. See also English (2016a).
6. On this point, see Rømer (2010), especially pp. 141–143.
7. This relates to what German philosopher, J. F. Herbart calls a one-sided person; they always see the old in the new, which means they frame things so that they fit prior conceptions of truth. He contrasts this with the multi-faceted person who can learn from new experiences. (Herbart, 1806/1902; see also English, 2013, p. 20).

8. Dewey's other related notion of imagination that Fesmire (2003) discusses is 'the creative tapping of a situation's possibilities' which is connected to 'empathetic projection', but more a part of addressing moral dilemmas in the context of action.
9. This move is in line with Fesmire's (2003) analysis of Dewey's term, see pp. 65, 66. This terminological switch from certain uses of the word 'sympathy' to contemporary uses of empathy is now more common since the terms have traditionally been associated with one another, and conceptual clarity about their distinctions is often needed with each usage, for example, Clohesy (2013) in citing Warnock's use of 'sympathy' says she is speaking of what he refers to as 'empathy'. p. 82.
10. On the connection between imagination and thinking, see Greene (1995) and Rømer (2010), especially pp. 141, and 143–148.
11. See Dewey's concept of growth, e.g. in Chapter 4 of Democracy and Education (1916/2008).
12. While intuitively it seems that it would be more easier to empathise with others more familiar with oneself, this is also now supported by recent psychological, neuroscientific research, which shows that acts of empathising with others with whom one knows less, and assumes is very different than oneself, is more difficult than empathising with those one views as more similar (Coplan, 2011, pp. 13, 14).
13. In several of her writings, Nussbaum has articulated 10 central human capabilities which she considers essential for a life lived with dignity. Imagination is part of one of these central capabilities, which she describes as 'Senses, Imagination and Thought: Being able to use the senses, to imagine, think and reason—and to do these things in a "truly human" way, a way informed and cultivated by an adequate education, including and by no means limited to literacy and basic mathematical and scientific training' (Nussbaum, 2006, pp. 75, 76).
14. Here, Nussbaum is referring to children gaining a sense of wonder through stories, but as a principle of how the narrative arts work to cultivate imagination, the principle applies to people of any age.
15. See Gadamer (1988) who describes this idea of empathy, p. 69. See also von Wright (2002).
16. Walter Benjamin was born in Germany, and lived from 1982 to 1940. His autobiography was written during the years 1932–1938 when he was living in exile (Benjamin, 2002).
17. This difference is not simply due to linguistic ability, although that can of course be a contributing factor. But, there are other reasons for this phenomenon, one main one being that in cross-cultural contexts, students and teachers can be guided by different norms and values, including those that function in the daily operations of classrooms, such as notions of the role of teacher, the role of students and associated ideas of authority or respect that have consequences for when a person feels it is right to speak and when it is right to listen.
18. What I mean by 'self-identified' is that the students referred to themselves as Muslim during the course.
19. I say this because of the more personal kinds of sharing that took place over time, and also because of interests shown to continue to study with me, among other things.
20. In an interesting discussion of space, Marginson (2010) discusses how creating 'space' is connected to imagination: 'Space is plastic…In many respects the spatial form that we inhabit are brought into being by human activities: by our imaginings and productions, by the ways we organise and govern ourselves' (p. 155).
21. Although my purpose in this paper was not to discuss assessment, I can say that some of these assignments are assessed, while others serve the purpose of fostering in-class discussion. Ryan (2012) gives a very insightful discussion of how providing students with opportunities for discursive and performative (including dance, music and drama) modes of reflection can help them connect to the discipline in higher education courses. She also discusses how to assess these modes of reflection. She argues that providing students to demonstrate reflection through diverse modes gives each student a chance to showcase individual communicative strengths.

22. On this point, see Burbules (2007), who discusses the productive spaces of the 'in-between' that are created between teachers' intentions and students' interests and which constantly need to be 'renegotiated' and can 'never rest static'. This idea is part of Burbules several works on doubt and the in-between.
23. I would like to thank the following colleagues for conversation we have had that have facilitated my thinking in this paper: Mordechai Gordon, Leonard Waks, Morwenna Griffiths, Carolin Kreber, Sue Chapman, Holly Linklater, Steven Fesmire, Neda Forgani-Arani, Stefan Hopmann, Dietrich Benner, Timothy Lensmire and all the participants who provided feedback at my talks. I would also like to thank the blinded reviewers for their thoughtful feedback on the paper.

References

Alexander, T. (1993). John Dewey and the moral imagination: Beyond Putnam and Rorty toward a postmodern ethics. *Transactions of the Charles S. Peirce Society, 29,* 369–400.
American Council on Education. (2015). *Internationalizing higher education worldwide: National programs and policies.* Washington, DC: Author.
Benjamin, W. (2002). Berlin childhood around 1900. In *Walter Benjamin: Selected writings* (Vol. 3, pp. 344–413). Cambridge: Belknap Press.
Boostrom, R. (2014). The dangers of imagination. In D. A. Breault & R. Braeult (Eds.), *Experiencing Dewey: Insights for today's classrooms* (pp. 91–92). New York, NY: Routledge.
Britzman, D. (1991). *Practice makes practice: A critical study of learning to teach.* New York, NY: SUNY Press.
Burbules, N. C. (2007). *Doubt and educational opportunity.* Retrieved August 18, 2007, from http://faculty.ed.uiuc.edu/burbules/papers/dep.html
Clohesy, A. M. (2013). *Politics of empathy: Empathy, solidarity, recognition.* Abingdon: Routledge.
Coplan, A. (2011). Understanding empathy: Its features and effects. In A. Coplan & P. Goldie (Eds.), *Empathy: Philosophical and psychological perspectives* (pp. 3–18). Oxford: Oxford University Press.
DBIS. (2016). *Teaching excellence framework. Technical consultation for year two.* London: Author
Dewey, J. (1916/2008). Democracy and education. In J. A. Boydston (Ed.), *The collected works of John Dewey: The middle works* (Vol. 9). Carbondale: Southern Illinois University Press.
Dewey, J. (1925/2008). Experience and nature. In J. A. Boydston (Ed.), *The collected works of John Dewey: The later works* (Vol. 1). Carbondale: Southern Illinois University Press.
Dewey, J. (1934/2008). Art as experience. In J. A. Boydston (Ed.), *The collected works of John Dewey: The later works* (Vol. 1). Carbondale: Southern Illinois University Press.
Dewey, J., & Tufts, J. (1908/2008). Ethics. In J. A. Boydston (Ed.), *The collected works of John Dewey: The middle works* (Vol. 5). Carbondale: Southern Illinois University Press.
English, A. R. (2013). *Discontinuity in learning: Dewey, Herbart, and education as transformation.* New York, NY: Cambridge University Press./mixed-citation>

English, A. R. (2016a). Dialogic teaching and moral learning: Self-critique, narrativity, community and 'blind spots'. *Journal of Philosophy of Education*, 50, 160–176. doi: 10.1111/1467.9752.12198.

English, A. R. (2016b, in press). The in-between of learning: (Re)valuing the process of learning. In P. J. Cunningham & R. Heilbronn (Eds.), *Dewey in our time: Learning from John Dewey for transcultural practice*. London: Institute of Education Press.

EPEC. (2006). Recommendation of the European parliament and of the council. *Official Journal of the European Union*. Retrieved May 20, 2016, from http://eur-lex.europa.eu/legal-content/EN/TXT/?uri=CELEX:32006H0962.

Fesmire, S. (2003). *John Dewey and moral imagination: Pragmatism in ethics*. Bloomington: Indiana University Press.

Gadamer, H.-G. (1988). On the circle of understanding. In J. M. Connolly & T. Keutner (Eds.), *Hermeneutics versus science? Three German views* (pp. 68–78). Notre Dame: University of Notre Dame Press.

Gallo, D. (1994). Educating for empathy, reason and imagination. In K. Walters (Ed.), *Rethinking reason: New perspectives in critical thinking* (pp. 43–60). Albany, NY: Teachers College, SUNY Press.

Greene, M. (1995). *Releasing the imagination: Essays on education, the arts, and social change*. New York, NY: Jossey-Bass Publishers.

Griffiths, M. (2014). Encouraging imagination and creativity in the teaching profession. *European Educational Research Journal*, 13, 117–129.

Hénard, F., & Roseveare, D. (2012). *Fostering quality teaching in higher education: Policies and practices*. Report of the OECD. Retrieved January 15, 2016, from https://www.oecd.org/edu/imhe/QT%20policies%20and%20practices.pdf

Herbart, J. F. (1806/1902). The science of education. In *The science of education, its general principles deduced from its aim, and the aesthetic revelation of the world*. (H. M. Felkin & E. Felkin, Trans., pp. 78–276). Boston, MA: D. C. Heath & Co.

Higher Education Academy. (2014). *Internationalising higher education framework*. London: HEA.

Higher Level Group on the Modernisation of Higher Education. (2013). *Report to the European commission on improving the quality of teaching and learning in Europe's higher education institutions*. Retrieved January 15, 2016, from http://ec.europa.eu/education/library/reports/modernisation_en.pdf

Marginson, S. (2010). World. In P. Murphy, M. A. Peters, & S. Marginson (Eds.), *Imagination: Three models of imagination in the age of the knowledge economy* (pp. 139–165). New York, NY: Peter Lang.

Nussbaum, M. C. (1997). *Cultivating humanity. A classical defence of reform in liberal education*. Cambridge: Harvard University Press.

Nussbaum, M. C. (2006). *Frontiers of justice. Disability, nationality, species membership*. Cambridge: Harvard University Press.

Prinz, J. (2011). Is empathy necessary for morality? In A. Coplan & P. Goldie (Eds.), *Empathy: Philosophical and psychological perspectives* (pp. 211–229). Oxford: Oxford University Press.

Rømer, T. A. (2010). Imagination and judgment in John Dewey's philosophy: Intelligent transactions in a democratic context. *Educational Philosophy and Theory*, 44, 133–150.

Ryan, M. (2012). Conceptualising and teaching discursive and performative reflection in higher education. *Studies in Continuing Education*, 34, 207–223. doi:10.1080/0158037X.2011.611799

Smith, M. (2011). Empathy, expansionism, and the extended mind. In A. Coplan & P. Goldie (Eds.), *Empathy: Philosophical and psychological perspectives* (pp. 99–117). Oxford: Oxford University Press.

von Wright, M. (2002). Narrative imagination and taking the perspective of others. *Studies in Philosophy and Education*, 21, 407–416.

American philosophy and its Eastern strains: Crisis, resilience, and self-transcendence

Naoko Saito

Abstract

This paper will critically reconsider the potential of Dewey's pragmatist idea of security without foundation. There is some potential in his anti-foundationalism as a form of wisdom for living beyond the risk society. I shall argue that Deweyan critical thinking needs to be further reconstructed, and even to be destabilized, if it is to exercise its best possible power of transcendence. One way to do this is to open its boundaries towards the 'East', towards European poststructuralism as well as towards East Asia, thereby destabilizing and transcending the limit of pragmatism. And I propose to do this through the mediation of Stanley Cavell's rereading of Emerson's and Thoreau's American transcendentalism.

The quest for certainty is a quest for a peace which is assured, an object which is unqualified by risk and the shadow of fear which action casts.—
John Dewey, *The quest for certainty* (1929)

1. Introduction: American philosophy in response to the challenge of the risk society

Ulrich Beck in his book, *Risk Society* (Beck, 1986/1992), provides us with a sense of the dystopia of postmodern and postindustrial society: we live within a complicated network of risks, whose ramifications were produced by human beings but go beyond human control. But risk management and minimization do not guarantee security. The center of 'risk consciousness' lies in the future (Beck, 1986/1992, p. 34), that is to say, in what is yet to be and, hence, is invisible here and now. Indeed, the social impetus of risks involves fear towards what is not present yet: oftentimes risks are unpredictable, while at the same time, invisible, and pervasive. The risk society is thoroughly negative and defensive as it orients us to a 'solidarity motivated by anxiety' (p. 49). The more anxiety increases, the greater the drive towards risk management—as if to cover over our fear. The danger of the risk society, as Beck reminds us, is that it is only we, human beings, who can convert the dystopia of the risk society into a hope for human solidarity. This requires overcoming the dichotomy between security and insecurity, and learning to persevere constantly in the process of converting instability to stability. In other words, whether we can achieve the utopia of the risk society hinges on human power and on its potential for converting risk to *crisis*—crisis as a chance, the momentum of conversion. In order for us to exercise the radical power of conversion, we need to reconsider the nature of 'critical thinking'—so that we can live not only in the risk society, but also *beyond* the risk society.

In response to this challenge, this paper will critically reconsider the potential of Dewey's pragmatist idea of *security without foundation*. There is some potential in his antifoundationalism as a form of wisdom for living beyond the risk society. I shall argue that Deweyan critical thinking needs to be further reconstructed, and even to be destabilized, if it is to exercise its best possible power of transcendence. One way to do this is to open its boundaries towards the 'East', towards European poststructuralism as well as towards East Asia, thereby destabilizing and transcending the limit of pragmatism. And I propose to do this through the mediation of Stanley Cavell's rereading of Emerson's and Thoreau's American transcendentalism. It is contended that Cavell's antifoundationalism can elucidate pragmatism's, and more broadly, American philosophy's *Eastern strains*, its troubled inheritance from Europe. This alternative path will show that mutually beneficial comparison can be conducted in a way that is indirect. Cavell's reinterpretation of American transcendentalism will engage us in a radical replacement: this is a replacing that places differently both of the human subject of and philosophy. It will reinforce American philosophy's antifoundationalism through the elaboration of a distinctive sense of transcendence—*transcendence in the ordinary*. This directs us downwards, to the ordinary, on the one hand, and upwards, towards the horizon of an excess beyond reciprocity and mutuality. This is critical thinking via transcendence—of a kind that is more radically risk-taking and, hence, more critical than Dewey's pragmatism in respect of the possibility of living *beyond* the risk society. I shall argue that such critical reconstruction is necessary to make best use of the wisdom of Dewey's 'security without foundation'.

2. Taking a further risk with pragmatism

Dewey's pragmatism is relevant in response to the challenge posed by the risk society. In *Experience and Nature* (1925), Dewey points us to the idea of security without foundation. His metaphysics of nature has the implication for us to rethink how we should live in the risk society. Risk taking *is* the condition of critical thinking—which is the very source of Dewey's experimentalism: in his words, 'Act, but act at your peril' (Dewey, 1984a, p. 6). By contrast, the mentality of 'safety first' puts an emphasis on pure thinking and knowledge over making and doing (ibid.). The source of our 'happiness' is derived from 'happenings' (Dewey, 1981, p. 45)—and etymologically 'hap' means chance, with 'happiness' originally implying something more like luck.

True happiness is to be attained by accepting the risks in action. When he says, '[a]t any moment the extraordinary might invade the commonplace and either wreck it or clothe it with some surprising glory' (Dewey, 1984a, p. 9), Dewey suggests something of the experience of transcendence in the common. His pragmatism implies that such transcendence requires critical thinking. In view of the etymologically common root of the words, 'critical' and 'crisis', we might say that pragmatism is a philosophy for converting crisis to happiness.

Dewey's idea of thinking cannot be simply contained in this stereotypical mode of problem-solving. It is best shown in his recounting of critical thinking. Dewey says that a key to creative activity is criticism (Dewey, 1984b, p. 143). His idea of the 'criticism of criticisms' (Dewey, 1981, p. 298) is, on Hilary Putnam's account, a matter of 'higher-level criticism', involving '"standing back" and criticizing even the ways in which we are accustomed to criticize ideas, the criticism of our ways of criticism' (Putnam, 2004, p. 96). Criticism of criticisms is to be distinguished from analytical thinking oriented towards clarity. Rather, it involves the robust power of thinking thoroughly in the uncertainty of life. Critical thinking entails, as a precondition of problem-solving, the existential question of how human beings can convert crisis into a chance to be taken. It is risk-taking by nature, involving an awakening to what has not been thought before, an adventure into the realm of the unknown. In *Art as Experience* (1934), Dewey calls this comprehensive notion of thinking 'creative intelligence'—a kind of thinking that integrates reason with emotion and imagination (Dewey, 1987, p. 351). Such a broader and higher form of thinking is already found in Emerson's and Thoreau's American philosophy. In what Cavell calls Emerson's 'thinking as thanking' (anticipating Heidegger), passion and patience are taken as keys to enhancing critical thinking beyond problem-solving (Cavell, 1990, p. 39; 1992, p. 132). This involves our realizing what our need needs, and this is not a matter of applying but of *receiving* intelligence (Cavell, 1990, p. 20).

Furthermore, thinking beyond problem-solving requires a peculiar mode of thinking—thinking in 'middle term' (Dewey, 1983, p. 96): American philosophy entails the possibility of opening a third way of thinking—a form of antifoundationalism beyond the dichotomy between foundationalism and non-foundationalism. In order to adventure into 'genuine uncertainty', Dewey takes *chance* to be the crucial element. Taking a chance, the moment of the leap, is at the heart of his experimentalism and philosophy for action. To think without fixed ground does not mean that anything goes. This is best illustrated by Emerson's idea of finding as founding. As Cavell remarks of his own approach to this: 'The step I am taking here is to receive the work of "Experience" as transforming or replacing founding with finding and to ask what our lives would look like if the work is realized' (Cavell, 1989, p. 109). This is an idea of perfection without final perfectibility, without abrogating the quest for a better life.

Under the auspices of risk management discourse, however, and in order to transcend its dystopia and convert it to a more positive form of solidarity, Deweyan critical thinking needs to be further reinforced, and even to be destabilized so that it can exercise the best possible powers of its antifoundationalist strain of thinking. An example that illustrates such a need is Michael Sandel's adaptation of Deweyan method of deliberative democracy for justice (Sandel, 2011). Critical thinking based upon accountability, transparency, and articulation through reason has a tendency to cover over what is invisible, what cannot be said. A more radical means of transcending the risk than what is provided by pragmatist discourse or critical thinking is called for—not simply to cope with the risk society, but also to live *beyond* the risk society. This asks us to step back and reconsider the precondition of critical thinking. In other words, we need a further, more radical *replacement of the subject of philosophy*—reconsidering what it means for each of us to be a human subject, to be the subject of critical thinking, and how philosophy as an academic subject can be reconceived. Simultaneously, it means that pragmatism must reinforce its antifoundationalism. This is a challenge to Deweyean modes of critical thinking in terms of the degree of their risk-taking and the extent of their powers of transcending the dystopia of the risk society.

One way to test the degree of transcendence that is made possible in Dewey's pragmatism, and hence to tap further the potential of its antifoundationalism, is to open the boundaries of American philosophy in terms of its controversial and complicated relationship with its *East*. First and most obviously, the 'East' now calls to mind East Asia. In the development of pragmatism, this source of influence mostly faded in America. Certainly Dewey's visits to Japan were not a great success, although he found a more receptive audience in China (Saito, 2003). From that time until today, the influence has been mostly one way—from West to East. Second, and less obviously, the 'East' has a different, less-exotic significance for the development of American thought, in that it referred to the Europe it had come from. This figured not as an external contingent matter of interest, as was perhaps the case with East Asia, but as something necessary and partly internal to itself whose significance it remained a task to fathom.

To tap the best potential of their common attempt of antifoundationalism, I shall explore a way of reading the different traditions in a mutually beneficial way. More specifically, I propose to reorient the relationship between *American* philosophy and *European* poststructuralism by way of American transcendentalism. Chantal Mouffe and Paul Standish, respectively, help us take such a turn. In her edited collection, *Deconstruction and Pragmatism* (1996), Mouffe attempts to explore the way in which 'Derridarian deconstruction and Rortyian pragmatism could contribute to the elaboration of a non-foundationalist thinking about democracy' (p. 2). Simultaneously, Mouffe points out the limitation of Rorty's Deweyan pragmatism, claiming that he acquiesces in the position that 'the conflict between fundamental values can never be resolved' (p. 6). Rorty cannot accept Derrida's 'quasi-transcendental reflection' and 'metaphysical questioning', aligning himself by contrast with pragmatism's engagement in 'real political issues' (p. 7). It is in this context of comparison that Mouffe introduces an alternative American lens, which, she thinks, better 'dovetails with' Derrida's deconstruction—Stanley Cavell's 'problematizating of the very idea of consensus' (p. 9). Siding with Cavell's criticism of Rawls, Mouffe says that '[Cavell] shows how deprivation of a voice in the conversation of justice can be the work of the moral consensus itself' (p. 10). Hinting at a breach within American philosophy, Mouffe suggests that pragmatism—especially if it is *Rortyian* pragmatism—is not the only way of representing American philosophy.

Likewise Standish's essay, 'Europe, Continental philosophy and the philosophy of education' (2004) focuses on a richer potential of the poststructuralism that has originated in Europe. Occasional, significant references are made to 'multiple influences' or 'cross-fertilizations' emanating from North America—especially from Emerson and Dewey (p. 500). While 'Nietzsche was influenced by Emerson and Thoreau and they in their turn by Asian thought' (p. 488), these apparently very different ways of thinking are alike 'conditioned by antifoundationalism' (p. 491), in pursuit of a commonality but without falling into the nihilistic relativism. To tap the potential strengths of their respective forms of antifoundationalism, some more nuanced deliniation is needed than crude distinctions between two geographical areas, say, between 'Europe' and 'North America', or between such questionable categories as 'continental' and 'Anglo-American'. Here Standish suggests the possibility of re-reading Nietzsche, Levinas, and Derrida in relation to the alternative voices of American philosophy—those of Emerson's and Cavell's (p. 490). Standish detects two (interrelated) streams of thought in both poststructuralism and American philosophy, and he names these as *affirmation* and *negativity*. Affirmation is a line of thinking that connects the strain of Nietzsche, Deleuze, and Lyotard with Emerson (p. 497). Negativity is a line of thinking associated with negative theology, with its focus on the infinite relation to the Other and on the idea of humility, potentially connecting Levinas with Cavell (and Emerson and Thoreau) (p. 495). Both streams follow the antifoundationalist view of language and, hence, both help to reconfigure the relationship between the inner and the outer, and between the private and the public. In this light, Mouffe and Standish together lay the ground for a different way of bridging American and European philosophies in order further to enhance the possibilities of antifoundationalism. They both indicate that it is Cavell who can open this alternative path of dialogue.

3. Cavell's antifoundationalism: Destabilizing Dewey's pragmatism

Cavell's blend of American and ordinary language philosophy is *cross-cultural* by nature, and his way of philosophizing opens up the boundary of American philosophy. It shows us an alternative way of antifoundationalism such as to destabilize and enhance Dewey's wisdom of security without foundation. First, Cavell has been engaged in a lifelong endeavor to bridge Anglo-American (Austin and Wittgenstein) and continental philosophy (Cavell, forthcoming). In his most recent autobiography, Cavell restates his sense that, with the dominance of analytical philosophy in the Anglo-American philosophical world, the voice of Emerson's and Thoreau's American philosophy has been suppressed and, hence, the philosophical voice he wants to hear (Cavell, 2010). He finds commonality between Emerson's and Thoreau's and Heidegger's 'thinking as thanking' (Cavell, 1992, p. 132). Yet in *The Philosophy the Day After Tomorrow* (2005), in contrast to Heidegger's proclivity towards home, Cavell finds the distinctive tone of departure in Thoreau (Cavell, 2005).

Second, with regard to the European poststructuralism of Derrida and Levinas, Cavell keeps his sense of distance and maintains a certain reticence. In the article, 'Education for grown-ups, a religion for adults: Skepticism and alterity in Cavell and Levinas' (2007), Standish discusses Cavell's strange relation to Levinas—a relation that combines an obvious kinship in their thought *and* Cavell's sense of distance from Levinas. Although both respond to the question of skepticism that originates in Descartes, Standish points out that Cavell's concern is more with an 'infinite responsibility for myself, together, let us say, with finite responsibility for the claims of the existence of the other upon me' (Cavell, 2005, p. 144 quoted in Standish, 2007, p. 81), while in Levinas the focus is rather on 'my infinite responsibility for the other' (Standish, 2007, p. 81). In other words, Cavell replaces Levinas' infinite Other by Thoreau's and Emerson's sense of nextness and neighboring (ibid.). He appeals not to an infinite God, but to *my* responsibility to the other, which can be exercised within the limits of human finitude.

Third, not only beyond the bounds of America, Cavell's sense of distance is manifested *within* American philosophy, insisting as he does on the distance between Emerson's and Thoreau's transcendentalism and Dewey's pragmatism. Cavell, who tries to resuscitate the voice of Emerson and Thoreau, expresses a sense of resistance to any facile connection between their thought and pragmatism (Cavell, 1990, 1998, 2003). He distinguishes Emerson's 'mode of thinking' from Dewey's 'intelligence', saying that in Emerson, '[t]here is no middle way between, say, self-reliance and self-(other-)conformity' (Cavell, 2003, p. 9). He expresses frustration with Dewey's declaration that language *is* public and *is* shared: '[l]anguage is not, as such, either public or private' (Cavell and Standish, 2012, p. 157). Cavell is attuned to Emerson's 'middle' not as a point but as a movement of oscillation, one that never allows us to settle down, and hence puts us into deeper anxiety. The 'cross-cultural' already begins here with its intra-cultural manifestations. These multiple cross-cultural dimensions in Cavell's philosophy are interrelated in the mediation of American transcendentalism.

It is here that Cavell's distinctive senses of the East are revealed, perhaps in terms of what I am calling American philosophy's *Eastern strains*—its troubled inheritance from Europe and its audible, if still faint echoes of East Asian thought —'strain' here carrying the double connotation of 'tension' and 'element'. Emerson and Thoreau both were interested and influenced by Indian and East Asian thought. In 'Walden in Tokyo', Cavell makes it explicit that 'from the beginning of writing my book its composition has been associated in my mind with the relation between cultures, and not alone between America and Europe but between America and Asia' (Cavell, forthcoming).[1] His 'cross-cultural' approach, however, is nothing like 'East Asian studies', a comparative philosophy between East and West, and neither has it anything to do with that mystification of Eastern culture that is prevalent in the West.

Cavell takes the view that American anxiety in relation to Europe is internal to (hence, is repressed in) American thought. The inevitable, quasi-intrafamilial struggle with this has led to forms of repression that, if he is right, continue to affect America today. Anxiety about what America can become—both carrying the heritage of Europe and freeing itself from its past—is inherent in Cavell's conception of America, and this crucially conditions his philosophy. It is not in Dewey but in Emerson and Thoreau that Cavell hears this poignant sense of American anxiety. What, then, is it to speak of Eastern *strains*? In the first place, a strain is an element of common stock or breeding—in more muted terms, a characteristic. Such an understanding might prompt questions regarding possible commonalities between American philosophy and the two 'Easts' identified above, where connections with East Asia will probably be the more surprising and interesting ones to consider. But 'strain' of course also has this other sense, and here we might think of the *tensions* between American philosophy (including pragmatism) and these two 'Easts'. It is my view that tensions of this kind provide valuable provocations to further thought, perhaps enriching Dewey's pragmatism in the process.

Cognizant of the diverse implications of America's Eastern strains, Cavell's concern is in what happens as these paths of thought intersect: in how each of us is to confront such moments in reorienting our ways of thinking; how each moment may turn us around, so that we relearn how to go on. This is attested to by the fact that his book on *Walden* was written right in the middle of the Vietnam War—America's invasion into Asia—which contrasted so painfully with his humble search for a lost voice of America, for what America itself had suppressed, and for the recovery of what America had to be proud of (Cavell, forthcoming). Cavell's thought, along with Emerson's and Thoreau's, is directed towards East in the oath of this 'onward thinking', within a quasi- religious imaginary of 'The Way' (Cavell, 1992, p. 136).[2] He represents Thoreau as the philosopher of morning in pursuit of a new dawn, which is ever still to be arrived at and, hence, never fully to be achieved (Cavell, 2005, pp. 217, 221). The theme of 'This New Yet Unapproachable America' (Cavell, 1989), the 'finding as founding' of America is a crucial tenet of Cavell's American philosophy. In 'understanding' other cultures, and riffing on connotations of 'home' and 'base', Cavell's point is not to hit a 'homerun', to reach home base, but to be ready for a continual (sometimes interrupted) movement towards 'first base' (Cavell, forthcoming). It is to be ready for a kind of immigrancy of thought. This is the exemplification of Cavell's antifoundationalism, a philosophy on the way.

Cavell also distances himself from Derrida's poststructuralism. Cavell feels that in Wittgenstein and Austin, as in Emerson and Thoreau, 'the mood of philosophy begins in the street, or in doorways, or closets, anywhere but in philosophical schools' (Cavell, 1994, p. 63)—and he finds a difference in tone, and hence, in the mode of thinking, in Derrida's sustenance of the grandiose terms of metaphysics and Levinas' hyperbolic invocation of infinity.[3] Here he indicates *American* transcendentalists' replacement of the subject of philosophy—philosophy brought back to the ordinary, philosophy becoming 'a clinical problem as much as a critical one' (ibid.). This brings Cavell closer to Dewey. Cavell's sense of distance from Derrida is expressed in terms of a difference in the 'sound of philosophy' (p. 77): 'I seem to hear the traditions scrape as they pass each other' (p. 74). In his manner of comparison, Cavell neither assimilates Derrida into Emerson and Thoreau, nor thinks in terms of differentiating between the two. Rather, he is interested in how the sound of scraping can make us realize who we are. To hear the scraping is to be attuned to why it matters how things are said, why it matters how we account for the way we live—which tells us much about what is at the heart of his ordinary language philosophy.

4. Transcendence downwards, transcendence forwards

Cavell's antifoundationalism rejects the mindset of finding equivalences, for this will prohibit further thinking of the kind that is needed if the antifoundationalist potential in these writers is to be realized. Bearing in mind the multiple senses of 'the East', and through the lens of American transcendentalism, we might be guided to pragmatism's, and more broadly, American philosophy's Eastern strains. Cavell's cross-cultural approach is indirect, in that different cultures exist adjacently to one another, and yet at a curious distance. The sense of this can perhaps be captured in the oxymoron of 'disjunctive bridging', in a logic of the 'between'. Such a logic is very much at the heart of Dewey's antifoundationalism, evident in his recurrent reference to 'the medium' or to being 'in the middle term' (Dewey, 1983, p. 51). This is not to be understood as a kind of compromise or half-way house: it is crucial to Dewey's pragmatist dynamic world view that, as Scheffler says referring to Peirce, 'we begin in the middle of things' (Scheffler, 1974, p. 44). Cavell's Emersonian way of being in the middle, however, has shown that his mode of thinking and use of language sustains *betweenness* of a more radical nature—in a way more thoroughly antifoundationalist than Dewey's pragmatism, always on the way.

Cavell's antifoundationalism comes to further light in the breached relationship between pragmatism and poststructuralism. He is a disturbing mediator on the part of American philosophy, in that the idea of what constitutes 'American' philosophy is shifted, in consequence of which any clear categorization of American and European philosophy may lose its purchase. Putnam says: 'Cavell is the only living American *transcendentalist*' (my italics).[4] Cavell gets closer than Rorty to Derrida's 'quasi-transcendental* reflection' (my italics), and yet revives the unique standpoint of *American* transcendentalism.

Victor Ketenbaum objects to Cavell's criticism of the relation of Dewey's pragmatism to Emersonian transcendentalism. Against Cavell's claim that 'to repress Emerson's difference [from Dewey's pragmatism] is to deny that America is as transcendentalist as it is pragmatist', Kestenbaum argues that 'Dewey was "in struggle" with himself on behalf of an American culture that was and is "as transcendentalist as it is pragmatist"' (Kestenbaum, 2013, p. 14), and that it is the idea of the 'turbulent' (pp. 17, 19) that has its place in his *'paideia'* (p. 18), suggesting a greater affinity with what Cavell calls 'spiritual disorder' (p. 19). The turbulent, Kestenbaum contests, is for Dewey the 'human condition', on the basis of which 'criticism and appreciation' are made possible (p. 19). Dewey, like Merleau-Ponty, has 'respect for' and 'receptivity to' the 'absent', the 'indirect', the 'unseen' and the 'hidden' as the condition of determining what is visible and what happens (pp. 22–23). Thus, Kestenbaum contends that the experience of transcendence is possible in, or even crucial to, Dewey's pragmatism (p. 28) and, hence, that it goes further and deeper into human adversity, seeing this in terms other than problems to be solved (p. 26).

Truly, it is unfair to Dewey to say that he is never troubled or anxious. In order, however, for Dewey and for us to be able to exercise the radical power of critical thinking, so that we can convert the dystopia of risk into *crisis*, despair into hope, a more radical turn in the way of thinking and the language of transcendence is called for—beyond the level of being satisfied with what is 'asserted', and of conceding that Dewey *is* troubled and that his metaphysics *has* its own turbulence. It is in their alertness to the performative aspect of language—to the way that to say something is to do something—that Cavell finds the radical difference in Emerson's and Thoreau's transcendentalism. Cavell says that the transcendentalism of Emerson and Thoreau is underwritten by ordinary language philosophy (and, by implication, that language plays a crucial role in transcendence) (Cavell, 1984, p. 32). It calls for the returning of language to the low, to the ordinary: this is a 'transcendence down' (Standish, 2012, p. 25). What we mean by 'transcendence' and how it takes place in the 'ordinary', in our re-engagement with language, is then the central issue to be addressed.

Cavell's redefinition of transcendentalism has multiple implications for its unique sense of antifoundationalism, and hence, opens up the scope of American philosophy beyond Dewey's pragmatism. It evokes a movement *onward*, not the upward movement symbolized by the attractions of Plato's sun (Cavell, 1990, p. 10, 1992, p. 136). By highlighting the adverbial phrase in Emerson's remark, 'the inmost *in due time* become the outmost' (Emerson, 2000, p. 132; italics added), with its implications of provisionality, uncertainty, and unpredictability, Cavell reminds us that the path from the private to the public is always still *to be achieved*. Transcendence down has another implication: of the sense of *shame*. Cavell perceives Emerson's idea of self-reliance as a 'study of shame' (Cavell, 1990, p. 47). The good society depends on 'me', involving my confrontation with the 'sins of society' (Cavell and Standish, 2012, p. 162) and my self-reproach (Cavell, 2004, p. 187, quoted in (Cavell and Standish, 2012, p. 173). This is a risk-taking beyond the secure discourse of the politics of recognition (Cavell and Standish, 2012, pp. 163, 173-174, nn. 12–16). Unlike Rawlsian conceptions of justice, you are never above reproach, and, hence, democracy is always still to come (p. 162). Furthermore, *language transcends itself*. Language is attached to the low and the common, and yet a certain spirituality is inherent in language, abundant in excess beyond human grasp. We find ourselves on 'some boundary or threshold, as between the impossible and the possible' (Cavell, forthcoming). This is symbolized by Thoreau's remark, 'The volatile truth of our words should continually betray the inadequacy of the residual statement. Their truth is instantly translated; its literal monument alone remains' (Thoreau, 1992, p. 217). Translation reveals an impulse to transcendence inherent in language, producing 'a new revelation within an old familiarity' (Cavell, forthcoming). Translation dispels routines at the same time as it demystifies transcendence.

Cavell says that Thoreau's 'philosophy of morning' is a book of *crisis* and that his *Walden* is 'writing about departure' (Cavell, 2005, p. 225). 'Morning' has, of course, the further connotation of 'mourning' (p. 217). As he rereads Thoreau's text to be 'about crisis and transformation, or metamorphosis' (p. 216), the focal point of transcendence is on the critical moment of conversion from negation to affirmation, as if realizing a 'philosophy the day after tomorrow'—a phrase designed to evoke the multiple significances of Nietzsche's '*Übermorgen*'—the day after tomorrow, the next morning, overcoming mourning and making possible a super-awakening (p. 118). The prefix '*Über-*', more than its English equivalent, itself suggests an exceeding of thought, which in turn reminds us of the overlapping of the inheritance of Emerson's Over-Soul in Nietzsche's *Übermensch*. The exceeding demands placed on us by these thoughts urge us to stand in the between.

5. Conclusion

Thinking on the way *is* difficult. To live thoroughly in an antifoundationalist way, these American philosophers express a precarious sense of standing on the border. Dewey says, 'Perfection means perfect*ing*, fulfillment, fulfill*ing*, and the good is now or never' (Dewey, 1983, p. 200, my italics). The call of Emersonian perfectionism is to perfect yourself here and now, to grasp the transient moment of the 'flying Perfect' (Emerson, 2000, p. 252), to set up the strong present tense against all the rumors of wrath, past or to come. (p. 316). Here is expressed a sense of taking a risk, being on the edge, in 'onward thinking' (Cavell, 1992, p. 135). This requires a way of thinking, of standing 'on tiptoe' (Thoreau, 1992, p. 71). As Thoreau says:

> In any weather, at any hour of the day or night, I have been anxious to improve the nick of time, and notch it on my stick too; to stand on the meeting of two eternities, the past and future, which is precisely the present moment; to toe that line. (Thoreau, 1992, p. 11)

Thinking on tiptoe is a key to sustaining a form of antifoundationalism that neither fully abrogates grounding nor fully relies on secure grounding. It will enable us to pursue risk-taking more radically, and, hence, to open the way to a more radical realization of the possibility of living *beyond* the risk society.

We need to cultivate a kind of critical thinking that self-transcendence is possible, such that we celebrate 'rebirth', converting risk to crisis (Cavell, 1992, p. 16). This calls for the cultivation of *the resilient self* along the lines of Emerson's 'Man Thinking' (Emerson, 2000, p. 44). The nature of resilience here is nothing like 'ataraxia' in Pyrrhonian skepticism or like Heideggerian 'resoluteness'. Rather, it involves a receptiveness to chance. Thinking can convert fate to power, 'the suffering of the necessity of action' (Cavell, 1994, p. 73). Cavell's reconfiguration of Emerson's and Thoreau's American philosophy through the lens of a 'transcendence down' elucidates the ordinary sense of the tragic, of sin and mourning, of depression and sadness, all as the part of the human condition, and, hence, as the essential condition for our critical thinking. This is a way of Emersonian thinking characterized by passion and patience (Emerson, 2000, p. 59; Cavell, 1990, pp. XXXVI; 20), where life is a source of thinking (Emerson, 2000, p. 51). Resilience is exercised and manifested in the moment of conversion, a kind of metamorphosis. Not only is this transcendence down, it is also *transcendence forward*—transcendence through the performative of a language that takes risks, acknowledging what Thoreau calls its 'extra-vagance' (Thoreau, 1992, p. 216). The vision of the resilient self presented here implies a kind of self-assurance that is different from the rational autonomous self. Such self-assurance is not self-centered, but rather is open to what happens, to chance and contingency. That is the only way to celebrate the 'happy hour', as Emerson says—the way to live beyond the risk society, to raise ourselves from fear and anxiety.

In *Democracy and Education* (1916), Dewey proposes the 'place of active occupations in education' (Dewey, 1980, p. 202). He says that play and active work in the curriculum are 'intellectual and social, not matters of temporary expediency and momentary agreeableness' (ibid.). Here 'knowledge-getting' is the result of actions and active occupations (pp. 203, 207). 'Outdoor excursions' are said to be not only useful by being social in their aims (p. 204). Dewey illustrates this by highlighting the experiences of gardening, hunting, and play (pp. 208, 210, 211). These ordinary activities can be the sites for learning to stand on tiptoe, fully persevering on the border between the inside and the outside. The experience of transcendence in the ordinary is a way of resisting the lure of foundationalism that today's global economy so easily proffers to us.

Disclosure statement

No potential conflict of interest was reported by the author.

Notes

1. Cavell says: 'the Bhagavad Gita is present in *Walden*—in name, and in moments of doctrine and structure' (Cavell, 1992, p. 117).
2. Hence he says: 'Emerson and Thoreau may be taken as philosophers of direction, orienters, tirelessly prompting us to be on our way, endlessly asking us where we stand, what it is we face' (Cavell, 1992, pp. 141–142).
3. Cavell says: 'Underlying the opposition to the metaphysical voice that I say Austin and Wittgenstein share with Derrida, there is all the difference between the worlds of the Anglo-American and the Continental traditions of philosophy' (Cavell, 1994, p. 63).
4. Private conversation on March 26, 2012 (Arlington, MA).

References

Beck, U. (1986/1992). *Risk society: Towards a new modernity*. (M. Ritter, Trans.). London: Sage.
Cavell, S. (1984). *Themes out of school: Effects and causes*. Chicago, IL: The University of Chicago Press.
Cavell, S. (1989). *This new yet unapproachable America: Lectures after Emerson after Wittgenstein*. Albuquerque, NM: Living Batch Press.
Cavell, S. (1990). *Conditions handsome and unhandsome: The constitution of Emersonian perfectionism*. Chicago, IL: University of Chicago Press.
Cavell, S. (1992). *The senses of Walden*. Chicago, IL: University of Chicago Press.
Cavell, S. (1994). *A pitch of philosophy: Autobiographical exercises*. Cambridge, MA: Harvard University Press.

Cavell, S. (1998). What's the use of calling Emerson a pragmatist? In M. Dickstein (Ed.), *The revival of pragmatism: New essays on social thought, law, and culture* (pp. 72–80). Durham, NC: Duke University Press.

Cavell, S. (2003). *Emerson's transcendental etudes*. Stanford, CA: Stanford University Press.

Cavell, S. (2004). *Cities of words: Pedagogical letters on a register of the moral life*. Cambridge, MA: The Belknap Press of Harvard University Press.

Cavell, S. (2005). *Philosophy the day after tomorrow*. Cambridge, MA: The Belknap Press of Harvard University Press.

Cavell, S. (2010). *Little did I know: Excerpts from memory*. Cambridge, MA: The Belknap Press of Harvard University Press.

Cavell, S. (Forthcoming). Walden in Tokyo (to be published in P. Standish and N. Saito (Eds.), *Stanley Cavell and the Thoughts of Other Cultures*.

Cavell, S., & Standish, P. (2012). Stanley Cavell in Conversation with Paul Standish. *Journal of Philosophy of Education, 46*, 155–176. May 2012 ('Interview').

Dewey, J. (1980). Democracy and education (1916). In J. A. Boydston (Ed.), *The middle works of John Dewey* (Vol. 9). Carbondale, IL: Southern Illinois University Press.

Dewey, J. (1981). Experience and nature (1925). In J. A. Boydston (Ed.), *The Later Works of John Dewey* (Vol. 2). Carbondale, IL: Southern Illinois University Press).

Dewey, J. (1983). Human Nature and Conduct (1922). In J. A. Boydston (Ed.), *The middle works of John Dewey* (Vol. 14). Carbondale, IL: Southern Illinois University Press.

Dewey, J. (1984a). The quest for certainty (1929). In J. A. Boydston (Ed.), *The later works of John Dewey* (Vol. 4). Carbondale, IL: Southern Illinois University Press.

Dewey, J. (1984b). Construction and criticism (1930). In J. A. Boydston (Ed.), *The later works of John Dewey* (Vol. 5 pp. 127–143). Carbondale, IL: Southern Illinois University Press.

Dewey, J. (1987). Art as experience (1934). In J. A. Boydston (Ed.), *The later works of John Dewey* (Vol. 10). Carbondale, IL: Southern Illinois University Press.

Emerson, R. W. (2000). *The essential writings of Ralph Waldo Emerson* B. Atkinson (Ed.), New York, NY: The Modern Library.

Kestenbaum, V. (2013). Dewey, *Paideia*, and Turbulence. *The Pluralist, 8*, 13–30. Spring 2013.

Mouffe, C. (1996). Deconstruction, pragmatism and the politics of democracy. In C. Mouffe (Ed.), *Deconstruction and pragmatism* (pp. 1–23). London: Routledge.

Putnam, H. (2004). *Ethics without ontology*. Cambridge, MA: Harvard University Press.

Saito, N. (2003). Education for global understanding: Learning from Dewey's visit to Japan. *Teachers College Record, 105*, 1758–1773. December 2003.

Sandel, M. (2011). *Michael Sandel Daishinsai Tokubetu-Kogi: Watashitachi wa Do Ikirunoka* [Special lecture by Michael Sandel on the earthquake in Japan: How should we live?]. Tokyo: NHK publishers.

Scheffler, I. (1974). *Four pragmatists: A critical introduction to Peirce, James, Mead and Dewey*. London: Routledge and Kegan Paul.

Standish, P. (2004). Europe, continental philosophy and the philosophy of education. *Comparative Education, 40*, 485–501. November 2004.

Standish, P. (2007). Education for grown-ups, a religion for adults: Scepticism and alterity in Cavell and Levinas. *Ethics and Education, 2*, 73–91. March 2007.

Standish, P. (2012). Pure experience and transcendence down. In P. Standish & N. Saito *Education and the Kyoto School of Philosophy* (pp. 19–26). Dordrecht: Springer.

Thoreau, H. D. (1992). Walden. In W. Rossi (Ed.), *Walden and resistance to civil government* (pp. 1–225). New York, NY: W. W. Norton & Company.

Why Should Scholars Keep Coming Back to John Dewey?

MORDECHAI GORDON

Abstract

This essay attempts to explain why philosophers, philosophers of education, and scholars of democracy should keep coming back to John Dewey for insights and inspiration on issues related to democracy and education. Mordechai Gordon argues that there are four major reasons that contribute to scholars' need to keep returning to Dewey for inspiration and guidance. First, is Dewey's pragmatic educational approach that seeks to maintain quality and stability in schools while rejecting the tendency to implement extreme changes in education based on the shifting winds of time. Second, Dewey's works contain both modern and postmodern elements and as such, it is difficult to label him as a member of one particular school of thought. Third, is the fact that Dewey's body of research represents a wide range of topics and interests from art to politics and from philosophy to the nature and purpose of education. Indeed, many of Dewey's essays and books can be viewed as a dialog between modern and postmodern ideas. Finally, and perhaps most important, Dewey's vision of democracy challenges us to recreate our global communities and our systems of education to meet the changing circumstances of history in such a way that all citizens (not just the wealthy or the powerful) can benefit.

Relatively few thinkers throughout history were trailblazers, ones who were ahead of their times and paved the way for others coming after them. Typically, these trailblazers raised critical problems and changed the terms of existing debates so that their followers could grapple with their questions and build on the answers that they provided. Sigmund Freud and Karl Marx are examples of such thinkers, who in the fields of psychology and sociology not only constructed concepts and theories that changed the conventional discourses in their respective disciplines, but also provided future scholars with a great deal of new territory to explore. Much like Freud and Marx transformed the disciplines of psychology and sociology, John Dewey revolutionized the field of education. As one of the fathers of the progressive movement in education, Dewey was able to imagine ways of teaching and learning that transcended the established norms of his time (based on rote and memorization) and to demonstrate connections between seemingly opposing elements. Throughout most of his life, Dewey grappled with the question of the relationship between education and democracy, but probably never in such a systematic way as he did in his book *Democracy and Education* (1916). Since then, many of the ideas that Dewey espoused about education and democracy and especially about the connections between the two have come under close scrutiny and critique. Nonetheless, numerous scholars of Dewey as well as philosophers and educators continually return to him for stimulation and guidance.

In this essay, I attempt to explain why philosophers, philosophers of education, and scholars of democracy ought to keep coming back to John Dewey for insights and inspiration on issues related to democracy and education. One hundred years after the publication of Dewey's *Democracy and Education*, it seems as though his ideas on a worthy education in democratic societies are as relevant as ever. In what follows, I propose that there are at least four reasons that contribute to scholars' need to keep returning to Dewey for inspiration and guidance. First, is Dewey's pragmatic educational approach that sought to maintain quality and stability in schools while rejecting the tendency to implement extreme changes in education based on the shifting winds of time. Second, is the fact that Dewey's works contain liberal and radical as well as modern and postmodern elements and, as such, it is difficult to label him as a member of one particular school of thought. Indeed, many of Dewey's essays and books can be viewed as a dialog between different ideological perspectives. Third, Dewey's body of research represents a wide range of topics and interests from art to politics and from philosophy to the nature and purpose of education. He provided thinkers with insights and food for thought on a variety of questions that are enduring in nature. However, Dewey's treatment of these diverse and complex topics is often dense and obscure, thereby opening up multiple avenues for interpretation. Finally, and perhaps most important, Dewey's vision of democracy challenges us to recreate our global communities and our systems of education to meet the changing circumstances of history in such a way that all citizens (not just the wealthy or the powerful) can benefit. He called on the citizens of democratic societies to imagine new ways of association and interaction that promote a respect for freedom, equality, and diverse ways of being in the world.

Educational Pragmatism

A brief glance at the last three decades of the history of education in the United States suggests that the field has experienced considerable shifts and changes during this time. Since I do not have the space in this article to give a comprehensive account of all of these transformations, I will only briefly mention a few of the events that have had the most impact on the field of education. For instance, during the last 30 years, we have witnessed debates on the viability of public schooling in the country, the emergence of magnet and charter schools as alternatives to traditional public schools as well as the taking over of public schools by privately run companies. During this time, we have also seen numerous curricular changes made and new programs launched in higher education in large part due to the demands of the economy and the need for a more skilled workforce. The last several decades also gave rise to the standards and accountability movement, which in turn led to the increased value placed on student performance, assessment, and standardized testing. And finally, we should not forget to mention the huge changes that have come about to the field as a result of the emergence of educational and communication technologies.

Much like our own situation, John Dewey lived through a time in which the winds of change were blowing through society in general and education in particular. In Dewey's case, he witnessed the emergence of the common school movement, which signaled the establishment of public schools throughout the country and the ability of more and more children to attend these schools. Additionally, Dewey observed the rise of vocational schools as institutions where boys and girls attended in order to get a useful trade for their future employment in society. And we should also note that Dewey took part in the heated debate between traditional and progressive education. Regarding this debate, Dewey made it abundantly clear in his book *Experience and Education* that extremes are dangerous in education and that progressives need to be careful not to throw out the good that the traditional approach had to offer:

> There is always the danger in a new movement that in rejecting the aims and methods of that which it would supplant, it may develop its principles negatively rather than positively and constructively. Then it takes its clew in practice from that which is rejected instead of from the constructive development of its own philosophy. (Dewey, 1938, p. 20)

What troubled Dewey about the controversy between traditional and progressive education was the risk of constructing a progressive approach to education that was based primarily on rejecting the tenants of traditional education rather than on developing and justifying its own principles. More fundamentally, in *Experience and Education* as well as in many of his writings, Dewey expressed his suspicion of *Either-Or* philosophies, of viewing the world in terms of dichotomous theories, and having to choose one side or the other while discounting any 'intermediate possibilities' (Dewey, 1938, p. 17). Indeed, Dewey was fascinated by the prospect of making connections between seemingly opposing viewpoints and of demonstrating how these connections can open up fresh (and more expansive) perspectives from which to consider education. One of his greatest contributions to the field of education, in short, is in his insistence on the need to take a broader and more complex view of age-old educational dichotomies such as the *child* versus *the curriculum*, *authority* versus *freedom* and *the individual* versus *the social*.

For instance, regarding the distinction between authority and freedom, Dewey wrote:

> The genuine problem is the *relation* between authority and freedom. And this problem is masked, and its solution begged, when the idea is introduced that the fields in which they respectively operate are separate. In effect, authority stands for stability of social organization by means of which direction and support are given to individuals; while individual freedom

stands for the forces by which change is intentionally brought about. The issue that requires constant attention is the intimate and organic union of the two things; of authority and freedom, of stability and change. (Dewey, 1925/1991, p. 131)

Dewey believed that the problem of authority has been traditionally addressed by assuming that it is diametrically opposed to freedom. In his opinion, this way of addressing the issue can get us nowhere and even contributes to the problem since it posits a theoretical gulf between the two. A much more fruitful approach, Dewey maintained, is to ascertain the relation between authority and freedom in experience in order to criticize it and suggest improvements. Dewey's point is that an adequate solution to the problem of authority has to begin by formulating the question differently: How is it related to freedom? This new question, he believed, will enable us to approach the issue from a broader and more holistic perspective and, therefore, discern alternatives that have not been possible to see before.

Indeed, scholars such as Jim Garrison have emphasized that Dewey favored a holistic approach to making sense of a variety of issues including metaphysics, scientific inquiry, and education. In his essay 'Realism, Deweyan Pragmatism and Educational Research', Garrison notes that:

For Dewey, experience was always experience of reality; there was no appearance-reality dualism. Experience could lead to false inferences if interpreted incorrectly; nonetheless, since human nature and experience are parts of nature, human experience was an adequate guide to the metaphysics of natural existence. (Garrison, 1994, p. 8)

The point that is relevant in our context is that Dewey's holistic approach in analyzing the natural environment as well as human culture continues to attract scholars, particularly ones who are troubled by more narrow, reductionistic attitudes and methods of inquiry. For these scholars, Dewey's holistic model is appealing in large part because they believe that it provides us with a complex and nuanced understanding of the world.

Returning now to the field of education and to Dewey's notion that extremes and either/or approaches are dangerous, we begin to grasp why scholars should keep coming back to Dewey. Take the issue of constructivist teaching and learning, a model that is commonly used in many educational institutions from preschool to higher education. One misuse of constructivist teaching is when teachers essentially require their students to teach themselves. Teacher candidates in my teacher preparation program spoke about professors who, after the first class meeting, divided the students into small groups and devoted the rest of the semester to having each group present to the class one or more chapters from the textbook. Several teacher candidates reported that 'they had learned nothing in this class' or that 'the professor had a very hands-off approach and did not really teach us very much'. To be sure, these students may be exaggerating when they claim that they didn't learn anything in the course. Still, it seems to me that there is a serious problem with the expectation that students teach themselves. While the constructivist notion that students should be encouraged to create their own interpretations of the text is a sound idea, this is not the same as leaving students to their own devices and requiring them to teach themselves. As Dewey warned us over 100 years ago:

> Nothing can be developed from nothing; nothing but the crude can be developed out of the crude – and this is what surely happens when we throw the child back upon his achieved self as a finality, and invite him to spin new truths of nature or of conduct out of that. It is certainly as futile to expect a child to evolve a universe out of his own mind as it is for a philosopher to attempt that task. (Dewey, 1902/1956, p. 18)

In this passage, Dewey reminds educators that an effective constructivist classroom is one in which there is a balance between teacher- and student-directed learning and one in which teachers take an active role in the learning process, including formal teaching. Similarly, with respect to the opposition between authority and freedom in education mentioned above, he emphasized that freedom cannot be simply identified with an absence of external controls. Instead, Dewey wrote that we need 'a kind of individual freedom that is general and shared and that has the backing and guidance of socially organized intelligent control' (Dewey, 1925/1991, p. 137). According to this view, intellectual liberty does not mean that one can say whatever one wishes (including racist or sexist comments), but rather that one can utilize one's freedom of speech and press to communicate ideas that enhance the common good.

My point is that one of the reasons that scholars ought to keep returning to Dewey for guidance and wisdom is that his call on educators to maintain stability and common sense while avoiding extreme fluctuations has proven to be correct. The field of education is one in which teachers, administrators, and other professionals are often forced to react to the changes that are happening in society or to implement mandates coming from the national and local governments. Historically, educators working in schools and classrooms in the United States have rarely been consulted about *what* they should be teaching students, *how* to teach basic skills, or *how* to assess that students are actually learning. Moreover, when educators are required to implement new standards and regulations they had no part in creating. they tend to give in and comply without putting up a fight. Dewey's approach can help remind educators that to merely vacillate from one side of the pendulum to the other in an effort to carry out the latest version of educational reform is misguided and can even be destructive for students. Remembering Dewey's counsel can enable educators to maintain a sense of direction and keep their eyes focused on what's most important to attend to in their work.

Building Ideological Bridges

Related to Dewey's holistic approach to resolving traditional educational dichotomies is the fact that it is really difficult to pin him down to one ideological position—ie liberal versus radical or modern versus postmodern. Let's consider for instance the debate between liberals and radicals on the nature of a democratic society. That Dewey was concerned with liberal values such as individual freedom and establishing strong community relations is well known. In his view, the legitimacy of a democratic regime does not rest primarily on the fact that it guarantees universal suffrage and other political rights. Rather, its legitimacy depends on its ability to provide the conditions in which the ordinary people have an opportunity to gather and debate on public matters. Dewey argued that the essential need in the American democracy

> is the improvement of the methods and conditions of debate, discussion and persuasion. That is *the* problem of the public. We have asserted that this improvement depends essentially upon freeing and perfecting the processes of inquiry and of dissemination of their conclusions. Inquiry, indeed, is a work which devolves upon experts. But their expertness is not shown in framing and executing policies, but in discovering and making known the facts upon which the former depend ... It is not necessary that the many should have the knowledge and skill to carry on the needed investigations; what is required is that they have the ability to judge of the bearing of the knowledge supplied by others upon common concerns. (Dewey, 1927/1991, pp. 208–209)

Thus, Dewey's writings clearly exhibited many of the principles of modern liberalism like a commitment to rational debate and persuasion as essential for the legitimacy of democracy.

However, it is equally difficult to deny the radical elements in his social and political philosophy. Dewey was a vocal advocate of participatory democracy in America and he rejected the dominant liberal-realist position which sought to minimize the power of the ordinary people and increase the responsibility of the powerful elite. As Robert Westbrook asserts, 'Dewey was a deviant among American liberals, a liberal steadily radicalized by his distinctive faith in thoroughgoing democracy' (1991 p. xvi). In fact, Dewey has more in common with modern radical educators such as Paulo Freire, Ira Shor, and Henry Giroux than is generally recognized. Like these radicals, he blamed the American schooling system for focusing on the wrong goals and for cultivating future citizens who lacked the capacity to discriminate and judge. And he insisted, like many radicals, that education has to be much more critical of itself than it currently is. His essay 'Education as Politics' provides a good example of Dewey's radical notion of democracy and of the power of schooling to bring about change in society. In this essay, Dewey called on educators to

> cultivate the habit of suspended judgment, of skepticism, of desire for evidence, of appeal to observation rather than sentiment, discussion rather than bias, inquiry rather than conventional idealizations. When this happens schools will be the dangerous outposts of a humane civilization. But they will also be supremely interesting places. For it will then have come about that education and politics are one and the same thing because politics will have to be in fact what it now pretends to be, the intelligent management of social affairs. (Dewey, 1922/1986, p. 334)

In addition to the fact that Dewey's conception of democracy includes liberal and radical elements, we should also note that his understanding of truth may be considered both modern and postmodern. On the one hand, Deweyan pragmatism may be rightfully regarded as modernist in the sense that he accepted various epistemological and ontological assumptions about nature. In their essay 'Deweyan Pragmatism and the Quest for True Belief', Christine McCarthy and Evelyn Sears make a strong case that Dewey's notion of truth and nature is ontologically realist. Drawing primarily on his book *Experience And Nature* (Dewey, 1929/1958), they write that his aim in this book 'is to employ in philosophy the method of empirical naturalism, and in so doing to bring to philosophy the myriad strength of modern science' (McCarthy & Sears, 2000, pp. 213–214). Indeed, Dewey himself acknowledged in *Experience and Nature* that his intention was to use the accepted methods of scientific inquiry to disclose the way in which we experience nature.

McCarthy and Sears point out correctly that Dewey accepted several assumptions of modern science such as the fact that both nature and the human world are constantly changing and that it is the task of science and philosophy to attempt to make sense of the processes and patterns of change. Challenging the notion that Dewey's view of nature is either idealist or radically constructivist, they cite the following passage from *Essays in Experimental Logic*:

> The position taken in these essays is frankly realistic in acknowledging that certain brute existences, detected or laid bare by thinking but in no way constituted out of thought or any mental process, set every problem for reflection and hence serve to test its otherwise merely speculative results. (Dewey, 1916, p. 35)

According to McCarthy and Sears, Dewey bought into the modernist view that it was the task of scientific inquiry to *discover* various objective truths about the natural world or human existence.

Although Dewey's conception of nature and scientific inquiry have modernist elements, it is difficult to deny that Dewey's epistemology and his understanding of truth as portrayed in such works as *The Quest for Certainty* and *Reconstruction in Philosophy* anticipate the postmodern view. For example, Richard Rorty readily admits that Dewey's antifoundational view of liberalism has been an inspirational source to him. In *Objectivity, Relativism, and Truth*, Rorty praises Dewey for 'debunking the very idea of "human nature" and of "philosophical foundations"' that liberalism and other traditional political theories have rested on (Rorty, 1991, p. 211). Echoing Rorty's position, Larry Hickman writes that Dewey is a postmodernist 'in the sense that he rejects the notion that there is some foundation of certainty on which we can stand' (Hickman, 2007, p. 20). For Hickman, the critical attitude toward traditional metaphysics espoused by many postmodern thinkers has already been established in large part by classical pragmatism.

Other Dewey scholars such as Stefan Neubert and Inna Semetsky believe that there are substantial affinities between pragmatism and the views of certain postmodern theorists like Michel Foucault, Gilles Deleuze, Felix Guattari, Jean-Francois Lyotard, and Jacques Derrida (Neubert, 2009; Semetsky, 2006). Neubert considers his efforts as part of the 'comprehensive and complex work of reconstructing Deweyan pragmatism' and establishing new links between Dewey's ideas and that of contemporary thinkers (Neubert, 2009; p. 355). Semetsky writes that the purpose of her book *Deleuze, Education and Becoming* is to 'address Deleuze's philosophy for the specific purpose of considering its potential practical effects and educational implications so as, ultimately, to make Deluze and Guattari's voice be heard in connection with what has been recently called the new scholarship on Dewey' (Semetsky, 2006, p. xxiii). Both Neubert and Semetsky are interested in forging a dialog between Dewey and various postmodern thinkers and exploring the different ways in which the two have mutual interests and intersecting concerns. As such, the research of Neubert and Semetsky falls into the category of border-crossing work, of research that transgresses traditional boundaries in order to make connections and open up new areas for investigation.

The fact that Dewey's writings exhibit both liberal and radical elements as well as modern and postmodern strands helps explain why researchers should keep coming back to him for stimulation and guidance. Unlike scholars whose positions are consistent and relatively uniform throughout their entire work, Dewey's views are not only multidimensional but evolved throughout his long life. My point is that the diversity and complexity of Dewey's theories can provide researchers with a rich source of ideas that are not only thought-provoking but also lend themselves to a variety of interpretations and uses based on the researchers' own interests. The issue that needs to be underlined is *not* that Dewey's philosophy is incoherent or inconsistent, but rather that its richness, diversity, and complexity have attracted and continue to attract scholars from a variety of disciplines and ideological perspectives.

Endless Possibilities

In the second decade of the twenty-first century, Dewey's writings continue to attract scholars in different disciplines from across the globe. Indeed, the breadth of scholarship on various aspects of Dewey's philosophy produced since the beginning of the new millennia is truly amazing. Recent books and articles written about Dewey are by no means limited to his ideas on education or pedagogy. On the contrary, these works deal with a variety of topics including esthetics, ethics, philosophy of science, social philosophy, religion, environmental philosophy, the connection between Dewey's ideas and Eastern philosophy, and much more. Take, for instance, Larry Hickman's edited volume *The Continuing Relevance of John Dewey: Reflections on Esthetics, Morality, Science, and Society*, which was published in 2011. As its title indicates, this book presents 'the views of internationally known scholars on some of the most important aspects of Dewey's work—in esthetics, ethics, philosophy of science and logic, and social philosophy' (Hickman, 2011, p. 1).

In one chapter of Hickman's book (in the section on *Esthetics*), Krzysztof Pitor Skowronski addresses Dewey's notion of esthetics in the context of the connection between the issue of power and esthetics. Interestingly, Skowronski finds relations between Dewey's work and *avant guard* artists such as Pablo Picasso and Marcel Duchamp and suggests that Dewey would agree that the arts can serve as a litmus test for the scope of liberty in a given stage of development of a given culture and society. (Hickman, 2011, p. 2) Another chapter in Hickman's book by Ramon del Castillo (in the section on *Ethics*) is titled 'John Dewey and the Ethics of Recognition'. In this chapter, Castillo distinguishes Dewey's political philosophy from Jurgen Habermas' communicative action theory as well as from the communitarian social philosophy that has been part of the debates on participatory democracy in the United States. The point that I wish to emphasize here is that contemporary scholars continue to find Dewey's views on esthetics and political philosophy relevant and his ideas provide them with food for thought on current debates in these disciplines.

Aside from the fields of esthetics, ethics, and political philosophy, current scholars have also produced exciting new research on the connection between Dewey and Eastern philosophy. For example, Joseph Grange's book *John Dewey, Confucius, and Global Philosophy* explores various relationships between Dewey's philosophy and Asian thought, especially that of Confucius. According to Grange, both Dewey and Confucius shared the conviction that human beings are not naturally good or bad, but must continually grow in order to become fully human (Grange, 2004, p. xv). For both, the social dimension of human existence played a primary role in their conceptions of human growth and development. Another important similarity between Dewey and Confucius is that both believed in the centrality of immediate experience for learning. As Grange writes:

> As is well known, Dewey insists on the importance of direct experience as the ultimate transformative agent. It is less well known that Confucius held a similar doctrine. The art of being human grows in direct proportion to our capacity to feel concretely the effects of our words and deeds. What we undergo and what we undertake has direct bearing on the temper of our personalities and the values that we hold. (Grange, 2004, p. xvi)

In illustrating some important connections between Dewey and Confucius, Grange hopes to initiate a conversation across diverse cultures and begin to bridge the gap between Western and Asian values.

The connection between Dewey's philosophy of education and theology is another topic that has received attention in the past few years. For example, Aaron Ghiloni's book *John Dewey Among the Theologians* challenges the conventional opinion that Dewey was no friend of theology and that his views were often 'anti-Christian' or 'atheistical'. Ghiloni's book presents a very different interpretation of John Dewey—'a Dewey whose insights provide the basis for substantive religious experience and vivid Christian thought' (Ghiloni, 2012, p. 1). Contesting the views of thinkers as diverse as Reinhold Niebuhr and Nel Noddings who tended to focus on Dewey's work *A Common Faith*, Ghiloni argues that 'it is possible to develop a constructive Deweyan theology by giving primary attention to Dewey's educational texts' (Ghiloni, 2012, p. 2). He maintains that texts such as *Democracy and Education, The School and Society*, and 'My Pedagogical Creed' contain an unexplored Deweyan theology.

One final example worth mentioning that illustrates the breadth of some of the new research on Dewey is Hugh McDonald's book *John Dewey and Environmental Philosophy*. The main purpose of McDonald's work is to defend Deweyan pragmatism from the charges of those critics who have labeled it as anti-environmentalist and anthropocentric. As opposed to these critics, McDonald argues that

> Dewey brings human nature back into nature as a whole, ending the isolation and detachment of the subject. Values are treated along with natural processes in a way that provides an alternative model for environmental ethics, one that is more closely in accord with the formal requirements of such an ethic. (McDonald, 2004, p. xv)

In McDonald's view, Dewey's naturalism serves as a counter-argument to those who would dismiss pragmatism as a whole for not being able to provide a foundation for environmental ethics.

This brief survey of the breadth of the research that has been conducted recently by scholars of Dewey is not meant to be exhaustive. Rather, my aim is to demonstrate that David Hansen is correct when he suggests that Dewey's writing contains as many possibilities as life itself (Hansen, 2006, p. 3). Although Hansen makes this point more specifically with respect to *Democracy and Education*, I think that his insight applies more generally to Dewey's entire body of work. The point is not merely that Dewey had eclectic interests and wrote on a variety of topics and questions that are perennial and fundamental to human existence, but that the way in which Dewey analyzed these topics and questions tends to leave the reader with many challenges and unanswered questions. For instance, Dewey's discussion of 'the public' in his book *The Public and its Problems* is rather ambiguous. Still, the ideas Dewey presented in this book—about one of the most pressing problems with the democratic society he lived through in the 1920s—are at once insightful and provocative.

The fact that Dewey's numerous and diverse writings tend to be not only provocative and insightful but also dense and opaque helps explain why scholars need to keep coming back to him for guidance and inspiration. An exhaustive and definitive account of Dewey's views on topics such as art, truth, nature, and democracy is very hard to come by. Much like the dialogs of Plato, it seems as though the answers that Dewey provided to the multiple subjects that he investigated are never conclusive and always stimulate additional problems. My point is that the complexity and ambiguity as well as the boldness of Dewey's ideas open up multiple avenues for interpretation and continually generate new areas for research. Indeed, when reading Dewey, one is left feeling that there are endless possibilities that need to be explored, plenty of questions that ought to be addressed, and countless connections that have yet to be made. For scholars of Dewey, this is good news and indicates that they are not likely to run out of issues to investigate any time soon.

Reconstructing Democracy

Thus far, my discussion has addressed the question of why should researchers return to Dewey's ideas and writings in general. In the final part of this essay, I wish to focus more explicitly on *Democracy and Education* and on why it makes sense for Deweyan scholars, educators, and other thinkers to revisit this work for guidance and insight. Even more specifically, I would like to examine why the notion of democracy articulated in this book as well as the integral connection that Dewey identified between education and a democratic society ought to continue to inspire contemporary scholars of these issues.

In order to address these questions, it would help to revisit the vision of a democratic society that Dewey expressed so eloquently in *Democracy And Education*. Chapter seven on 'The Democratic Conception in Education', famously includes the following:

> A democracy is more than a form of government; it is primarily a mode of associated living, of conjoint communicated experience. The extension in space of the number of individuals who participate in an interest so that each has to refer his own action to that of others, and to consider the action of others to give point and direction to his own, is equivalent to the breaking down of those barriers of class, race, and national territory which kept men from perceiving the full import of their activity. (Dewey, 1916, p. 87)

In this passage, Dewey is attempting to provide a deeper justification than the one usually given to the question of why a democratic society is devoted to education more than other societies. For Dewey, the conventional explanation—that the well-being of a democratic society rests on the electorate being informed about and engaged in public life—is grossly inadequate. More fundamental is that a democracy depends on two central principles: first, the citizens working together to promote interests that benefit the common good; second, the ability of individuals to consider the perspectives of those in society who are different from them before deciding how to speak and act. The development of shared interests and appreciation of diverse viewpoints, he believed, promote extensive interaction between individuals and prevent the society from becoming rigid and static. In short, Dewey insisted that a democratic society is one that depends upon and is strengthened by common associations and free interaction among diverse groups.

What is at stake here for Dewey is that common associations and free interactions enhance growth, that is, they lead the society to become more democratic. As Kathy Hytten writes, 'the more ideas and viewpoints we can consider as we make our way in the world and solve problems, the better chance we have of furthering knowledge, cultivating understanding and tolerance, and developing enriching social arrangements' (Hytten, 2009; pp. 398–399). In contrast, isolation and intolerance of others typically lead a society to stagnation or to become autocratic. Dewey recognized correctly that dialog, interaction with others, and the free exchange of ideas can help groups of people and humanity at large become more liberated and just. To be perfectly clear, when Dewey claimed that democracy is deeply devoted to education, he did not mean it in the *narrow* sense of education commonly used today—ie that it is committed to providing highly quality schooling for all of its citizens. Education was understood by him in the *broad* sense of the term to refer to any interaction among human beings in which information is exchanged, feelings are conveyed, or moral edification takes place. As Stefan Neubert suggests, Dewey believed that every genuine communication 'provides the participants within mutually shared relationships with opportunities to learn from each other's experiences' (Neubert, 2010, p. 488). Thus, a democratic society, according to Dewey, is one that is *committed* to promoting free and varied contacts among diverse groups of people and individuals.

Democracy And Education laid the foundation for Dewey's dynamic conception of democracy, which he developed more explicitly in some of his later essays. In the summary of chapter seven of this book, Dewey wrote that 'a society which makes provision for participation in its good of all its members on equal terms and which secures flexible readjustment of its institutions through interaction of the different forms of associated life is in so far democratic' (Dewey, 1916, p. 99). The notion of *flexible readjustment of its institutions* is key to understanding Dewey's concept of democracy and is one that he expanded on in some of his later works. For instance, in his 1937 essay 'The Challenge of Democracy to Education', Dewey argued that the greatest mistake one can make about democracy is to conceive it as something fixed rather than changing:

> The very idea of democracy, the meaning of democracy, must be continually explored afresh; it has to be constantly discovered, and rediscovered, remade and reorganized; while the political and economic and social institutions in which it is embodied have to be remade and reorganized to meet the changes that are going on in the development of new needs on the part of human beings and new resources for satisfying these needs. (Dewey, 1937, p. 182)

Hence, Dewey advocated a dynamic view of democracy, the notion that its meaning can never be something permanent and fixed. He insisted that the concept of democracy needs to be constantly reformulated and the institutions that support it need to be reconfigured in order to meet the changing social, political, economic, and technological shifts that are taking place in the world. Dewey's essay 'Creative Democracy: The Task Before Us' echoed the notion that democracy is an ongoing process of recreating and reorganizing society for the better. He wrote that 'the task of democracy is forever that of creation of a freer and more humane experience in which all share and to which all contribute' (Dewey, 1939, p. 229). In this essay, Dewey associated the idea of democracy with his notion of experience and suggested that both need to be evaluated on the extent to which they lead to *growth*, that is, to richer, more meaningful, and freer ways of living.

At this point, we can begin to see why scholars of Dewey as well as educators and other researchers would benefit by continually returning to his notion of democracy for guidance and inspiration. For Dewey, as John Shook argues, 'neither the capacities of the individual nor the needs of the community are known fixed matters, but these instead require endless readjustment to each other as they ceaselessly evolve' (Shook, 2013, p. 23). The point is that there is something very appealing about a notion of democracy that emphasizes the need to continually redefine the meaning of this concept and reconstruct the institutions upon which the idea rests to meet the changing circumstances of the time. Dewey's notion is attractive because it recognizes that our current form of democracy is not perfect and should be amended when new challenges emerge and when the social, political, and economic situations have shifted. According to this view, each new generation of citizens has an important role to play in reframing the idea of democracy and in adjusting the systemic foundations upon which it is based (ie revising obsolete laws and creating new support mechanisms). On my reading, Dewey challenged us and future generations to scrutinize his notion of democracy in order to critique this idea and make improvements to it.

Much like many of Plato's dialogs, Dewey invites us to engage with him and with ourselves in an ongoing conversation about the meaning of democracy and its connection to education.

Another important advantage of Dewey's notion of democracy is that it reminds us, as Kathy Hytten notes,

> of the importance of context, maintaining that democracy must emerge from the concerns, values, habits and practices of cultural groups. It is never something that can be imposed from above or achieved through non-democratic means, such as economic colonization or unjust war. (Hytten, 2009, p. 397)

Hytten's point is that Dewey's conception of democracy helps us realize that we must be extremely careful when attempting to apply concepts or institutions that were created in a particular context to a completely different set of conditions and circumstances. The reason is that the economic, social, and political context existing when ideas and institutions were developed had a significant impact on the nature of these ideas. Once the context is altered, it is fair to assume that the concepts and organizational structures will have to be changed as well. For this reason, documents such as the Constitution of the United States should never be considered 'sacred texts' that can never be challenged or amended. Learning from Dewey, we should conclude that since the social, economic, and political context in which the United States Constitution was drafted has changed dramatically, it stands to reason that we need to revise this document to meet the current state of democracy in this country.

Finally, I believe that what continues to attract scholars from a variety of disciplines to *Democracy and Education* is the symbiotic relationship that Dewey postulated between education and democracy, a relation not present in other forms of political systems. Of course one could argue that authoritarian political systems also tend to have an intimate relation to education, but, unlike democracies, the former are not committed to promoting free and varied contacts among diverse groups of people. Regarding the unique relationship relation between democracy and education, David Hansen writes that:

> Democracy can only exist if practice is reconstructed so that all persons can, in principle, realize their potential as human beings. Conversely, Dewey argues that the very idea of democracy is implied in the core understanding of education as reconstruction, as the continuous growth of all persons. (Hansen, 2006, p. 11)

Hansen's point is that there is an organic (to use a Deweyan term) relation between democracy and education in that each is dependent on and at the same time influences the other. To be sure, teaching and learning have existed and continue to take place in societies that are not democratic. But the kind of education that Dewey favored—one that helps each person grow and reach their full potential—can only exist in a society that puts a premium on individual liberty, citizens working together to achieve the common good, and on genuine respect for diverse perspectives and life styles (ie democratic).

The symbiotic relationship between education and democracy is itself something that needs to be *reconstructed* anew from time to time when the economic, social, and cultural conditions in a society change. That is, the promise of Dewey's conception is in the challenge that he left us—to continually reflect on how democracy can be reconfigured to better serve the development of individuals and how education can be improved to support the democratic system of organization. This challenge is ongoing and can never be fully realized since no education system or democratic society known to us has ever come close to being perfect. Reconstructing this relationship will require us and future generations to persist in the task that Dewey envisioned—to work individually and collectively to continually explore, revisit, and remake both democracy and education.

Disclosure statement

No potential conflict of interest was reported by the author.

References

Dewey, J. (1916a). *Democracy and education: An introduction to the philosophy of education*, New York, NY: The Free Press.
Dewey, J. (1916b). *Essays in experimental logic*. New York, NY: Dover Publications.
Dewey, J. (1922/1986). Education as politics. In J. A. Boydston (Ed.), *John Dewey: The middle works* (Vol. 13, pp. 329–334). Carbondale: Southern Illinois University Press.
Dewey, J. (1937). The challenge of democracy to education. In J. A. Boydston (Ed.), *John Dewey, The later works, 1925–1953* (Vol. 11, pp. 181–190). Carbondale: Southern Illinois University Press, 1987.
Dewey, J. (1938). *Experience and education*. New York, NY: Macmillan Publishing Company.
Dewey, J. (1939). Creative democracy: The task before us. In J. A. Boydston (Ed.), *John Dewey, The later works, 1925–1953* (Vol. 14, pp. 224–230). Carbondale: Southern Illinois University Press, 1988.
Dewey, J. (1929/1958). *Experience and nature*. New York, NY: Dover Publications.
Dewey, J. (1902/1956). *The child and the curriculum and the school and society*. Chicago, IL: University of Chicago Press.
Dewey, J. (1927/1991). *The public and its problems*. Athens: Shallow Press.
Dewey, J. (1925/1991). Authority and social change. J. A. Boydston (Ed.), *John Dewey: The later works* (Vol. 11, pp. 130–135). Carbondale: Southern Illinois University Press.
Garrison, J. (1994). Realism, Deweyan pragmatism and educational research. *Educational Researcher, 23*, 5–14.
Ghiloni, A. (2012). *John Dewey among the theologians*. New York, NY: Peter Lang Publishing.
Grange, J. (2004). John Dewey, Confucius, and global philosophy. Albany: State University of New York Press.

Hansen, D. (2006). *John Dewey and our educational prospect: A critical engagement with Dewey's democracy and education*. Albany: State University of New York Press.

Hickman, L. (2007). *Pragmatism as postmodernism: Lessons from John Dewey*. New York, NY: Fordham University Press.

Hickman, L. (2011). *The continuing relevance of John Dewey: Reflections on aesthetics, morality, science, and society*. New York, NY: Rodopi.

Hytten, K. (2009). Deweyan democracy in a globalized world. *Educational Theory, 59*, 395–408.

McCarthy, C., & Sears, E. (2000). Deweyan pragmatism and the quest for true belief. *Educational Theory, 50*, 213–227.

McDonald, H. (2004). *John Dewey and environmental philosophy*. Albany: State. University of New York Press.

Neubert, S. (2009). Reconstructing Deweyan pragmatism: A review essay. *Educational Theory, 59*, 353–369.

Neubert, S. (2010). Democracy and education in the twenty-first century: Deweyan pragmatism and the question of racism. *Educational Theory, 60*, 487–502.

Rorty, R. (1991). *Objectivity, relativism and truth*. Cambridge: Cambridge University Press.

Semetsky, I. (2006). *Deleuze, education and becoming*. Rotterdam: Sense.

Shook, J. (2013). Dewey's ethical justification for public deliberation democracy. *Education and Culture, 29*, 3–26.

Westbrook, R. (1991). *John Dewey and American democracy*. Ithaca, NY: Cornell University Press.

Index

Page numbers in *italics* refer to figures. Page numbers followed by "n" refer to notes.

activism: civic 13, 15–17; educational potential of 17–19
Adorno, Theodor 81
aesthetic experience *45*, *46*; and reflective experience *46*
affective thought 45
Alexander, Thomas A. 55, 59, 78
American democratic government 40
American pragmatism 64
American transcendentalism 90, 92, 94, 96
antifoundationalism 4, 90, 93–4, 96
Apple, M. W. 9
Arditi, B. 16
Arendt, Hannah 81
Art as Experience (Dewey) 74–5, 91
arts, teaching through 79–84
Ayers, W. 9

Barber, William 14
Beane, J. A. 9
Beck, Ulrich 89, 90
behaviorism 26; Skinnerian 28
Benjamin, Walter 81, 86n16
Bernstein, Richard 58
Biesta, G. 41
Boostrom, Robert 85
Brandom, Robert 58
Britzman, Deborah 84
Buddhism 57
Burbules, N. C. 87n22

capitalism 31
Castillo, Ramon del 108
Cavell, Stanley 4, 93–5; antifoundationalism 93–4, 96; cross-cultural approach 96; transcendentalism 97
chauvinism 33
children: acquisition of language 61; Dewey and philosophy for/with 64–6

Chomsky, N. 16
civic activism 13, 15–17
civil rights movements 13
classism 33
Clohesy, A. M. 86n9
'coherent theory of experience' 42–6, *45*, *46*; through occupations 47–8
Collected Works of John Dewey, The (Dewey) 50n1
Cologne interactive constructivism 34
colonialism 33
Common Faith, A (Dewey) 109
communication 28, 56–60; Dewey's philosophy of 62
complexity, as educational challenge 31–5
Continuing Relevance of John Dewey, The (Hickman) 108
criticisms 21–2; of reductionist approaches in education 22–8
cross-cultural approach, Cavell's 94, 96
cross-cultural understanding, creating 'third voice' to support 81–4

Deconstruction and Pragmatism (Mouffe) 92
Deleuze, Education and Becoming (Semetsky) 108
Deleuze, Gilles 107
democracy 2, 7–10, 15–17, 32; education for 7; and education, in era of globalization 1–4; habits of 10–12; John Dewey on 7–10
Democracy and Education (Dewey) 5, 7, 22, 27, 98, 102, 111; Dewey's philosophical emphasis in 41; experience and thinking 43; experiential heart of 37–41; occupations as living expression of 48–50
democratic education 2; ideas in 22
democratic governments 39–40
democratic schools 9; visions, for schooling 9–10
Derrida, Jacques 107

INDEX

Dewey, John 101; building ideological bridges 105–8; critical thinking 91–2; criticisms 21–2; and democracy 2, 7–10, 15–17; diversity of stimulation 11; educational legacy 66; education as politics 106; features of reflective experience 45; holistic model of 104; idea of thinking 91; imagination 75–9; model of inquiry, learning, and problem solving 29–30; naturalism 110; and philosophy for/with children 64–6; philosophy of democracy 32; philosophy of education 42; philosophy of language 58–64; possibilities for ideas of 108–10; pragmatism 4, 90–4, 97, 107; reconstructing democracy 110–14; scholarship 74; theory of learning 72; visits to Japan 92; vision of democracy 6, 7

Dewey's criticisms 21–2; of reductionist approaches in education 22–8

Duchamp, Marcel 108

Eastern strains, of American philosophy 3, 4, 90, 94, 95, 96

education: challenges, complexity and reductionism as 31–5; debates, reductionism in contemporary 28–31; for democracy 7; democratic ideas in 22; Dewey's criticisms of reductionist approaches 22–8; Dewey's philosophy of 42; Froebel's model of 24; legacy 66; potential of activism 17–19; pragmatism 102–5

educational theory 43

Education and Culture (2012) (Gregory) 67n5

'Education as Unfolding' 25

Elementary School Journal, The (Dewey) 41

Emersonian perfectionism 98

Emerson, R. W. 93, 95, 96

empathy: imagination and 77–9; imagination as projection of 79–84

English, Andrea R. 1, 70

Essays in Experimental Logic (Dewey) 107

esthetic experience 45, 46

European poststructuralism 4, 93

experience: coherent theory of 42–6, 45, 46; modes of 46; through occupations 47–8

Experience and Education (Dewey) 42, 103

Experience and Nature (Dewey) 59, 90

experimentalism 11, 90

fallibilism 63

Fesmire, S. 9, 86n8

Fitzsimons, Patrick 57

Forward Together Moral Movement 15, 17; in North Carolina 2, 7, 14

Foucault, Michel 107

Freire, Paulo 106

Freud, Sigmund 101

Froebel: approach 24; model of education 24; reductionism 24

Garrison, Jim 2, 21, 104

Gavin, Bill 34

genetic fallacy 27

Ghiloni, Aaron 109

Giddens, Anthony 57

Giroux, Henry 106

globalization 57, 58; John Dewey's democracy and education in era of 1–4; neoliberal, contemporary era of 13

Gordon, Mordechai 1, 4, 101

Gould, S. J. 35n2

Grange, Joseph 109

Granger, David 63, 67n6, 67n7

Greene, Maxine 54

Green, J. M. 6, 15, 19

Gregory, Maughn 63, 67n5–n7

Guattari, Felix 107

Hansen, David 54, 57, 110, 113

Harry Stottlemeier's Discovery (Lipman) 64

Hawken, P. 11

Haynes, Bruce 57

Hegel 25, 35n2; Hegelian theory 25

Herbart, J. F. 85n7

Hickman, Larry 107, 108

higher education 79–84; policy, implications 84–5; teaching, reform 71

How We Think (Dewey) 44, 55

Hytten, Kathy 2, 5, 57, 111, 113

imagination 75–7; as empathetic projection 79–84; and empathy 77–9

Institute for the Advancement of Philosophy for Children (IAPC) 67n7

'integral experience' 76

intellectualism 34

Islam 57

John Dewey Among the Theologians (Ghiloni) 109

John Dewey and Environmental Philosophy (McDonald) 109

John Dewey, Confucius, and Global Philosophy (Grange) 109

Journal of Education, The (Dewey) 41

Kestenbaum, V. 96

Kilpatrick, William Heard 54, 67n2

Kliebard, H. M. 41

K-12 schools 3, 54, 63

Kumashiro, K. 9

Kurth-Schai, R. 11

language: child's acquisition of 61; Dewey's philosophy of 58–64

Laverty, Megan 3, 53

INDEX

learning: Dewey's theory of 71, 72; exploring in-between of 72–9; role of imagination 72–9
Levinas 93, 94
Levine, Steven 58
Lipman, Matthew 63, 64, 67n7
Logic: The Theory of Inquiry (Dewey) 44
Lyotard, Jean-Francois 107

Marginson, S. 86n20
Marx, Karl 101
McCarthy, C. 107
McDonald, Hugh 109
Meiners, E. 9
meliorism, pragmatic 12
Merleau-Ponty 96
Mexico, Zapatista revolt in 13
Misak, Cheryl 58
Mouffe, Chantal 92

nationalism 33
naturalism 110
negativity 93
neoliberal globalization, contemporary era of 13
Neubert, Stefan 2, 21, 107, 108, 111
Nietzsche: *Ubermensch* 97; *Ubermorgen* 97
non-reflective experience 45; *see also* esthetic experience
North Carolina, Forward Together Moral Movement in 2, 7, 14
Nussbaum, Martha 3, 79–81, 86n13

Objectivity, Relativism, and Truth (Rorty) 107
Occupy Movement 2, 13, 14, 16

Papastephanou, Mariana 57
patriarchy 33
perfectionism, Emersonian 98
Philosophy the Day After Tomorrow, The (2005) (Cavell) 93
Picasso, Pablo 108
Pierre Cometti, Jean 58
PISA 29, 30
pluralism 11
poststructuralism, European 4, 93
pragmatism 64, 97, 107; American 64; destabilizing 93–4; Dewey and 4, 90–4, 97, 107; educational 102–5; risk with 90–3; *see also Deconstruction and Pragmatism* (Mouffe); meliorism, pragmatic
problem-solving 58
progressive education 54; educators 55
Public and its Problems, The (Dewey) 110

qualitative thought 45
Quay, John 2, 37
Quest for Certainty, The (Dewey) 107
Quinn, T. 9

racism 33
Reconstruction in Philosophy (Dewey) 107
reductionism 27; in contemporary educational debates 28–31; as educational challenge 31–5; Froebel 24
reflective experience 74; aesthetic experience and *46*; Dewey's general features 43–4, *45*, *46*
reflective learning experiences 74
reform, in higher education teaching 71
Reich, Kersten 2, 21
Risk Society (Beck) 89
Rorty, Richard 58, 107
Ruggerio, G. 14
Rushkoff, D. 16
Ryan, M. 86n21

Saito, Naoko 3, 4, 57, 89
Sandel, Michael 91
scholarship 74
School and Society, The 109
schooling, democratic visions for 9–10
Sears, E. 107
Selma-to-Montgomery march (1965) 14
Semetsky, Inna 107, 108
Sharp, Ann Margaret 64
Shea, James R. 58
Shook, John 112
Shor, Ira 106
Skinner box 26
Skinnerian behaviorism 28
Skowronski, Krzysztof Pitor 108
'Social and Civic Competence' 85n2
social Darwinism 31, 32; ideologies 33
social movements 12, 18; contemporary 12–15
Solnit, R. 11–13, 15
Standish, Paul 92–4
Stitzlein, S. 10
Stovall, D. 9
Studies in Logical Theory (Dewey) 44

Teaching Excellence Framework (TEF) 84
teaching, through arts 79–84
technicist thinking 58
'technological discoveries and inventions' 39
TEF *see* teaching excellence framework (TEF)
thinking, role of imagination in 72–9
Thoreau, H. D. 93, 95, 96, 98
transcendence: downwards and forwards 95–7
transcendentalism 90, 92, 94, 96, 97

Voting Rights Act 14
Vrba, E. S. 35n2

Westbrook, Robert 106

Zapatista revolt, in Mexico 13